GUIDING YOUNG

Curriculum Ideas for Teachers

GUIDING YOUNG ARTISTS

Curriculum Ideas for Teachers

Gaelene Rowe

OXFORD
UNIVERSITY PRESS

Melbourne

OXFORD UNIVERSITY PRESS AUSTRALIA

Oxford New York Toronto
Delhi Bombay Calcutta Madras Karachi
Kuala Lumpur Singapore Hong Kong Tokyo
Nairobi Dar es Salaam Cape Town
Melbourne Auckland Madrid
and associated companies in
Berlin Ibadan

OXFORD is a trademark of Oxford University Press

First published 1987
Reprinted 1987, 1988, 1989, 1991, 1993

National Library of Australia
Cataloguing-in-Publication data:

Rowe, Gaelene.
  Guiding young artists.

  Bibliography.
  ISBN 0 19 554804 3.

  1. Art—Study and teaching (Elementary). I. Title.

372.5'44

Acknowledgement
The author wishes to thank the kids of her family and
friends for the great drawings, and Judy Bowden for
the use of her photographs.

Designed by Steven Randles
Illustrations by Judy Green
Typeset by Midland Typesetters, Maryborough, Victoria
Printed in Hong Kong
Published by Oxford University Press,
253 Normanby Road, South Melbourne, Australia

CONTENTS

INTRODUCTION

LEARNING ART: PROCESS AND PRODUCT

As with any other human skill, the best way to 'learn' art is through use, to become immersed in it, to learn through trial and error. While many teachers may be prepared to accept this in theory, they may find the idea difficult to adopt in practice. Traditionally the emphasis in art teaching has been on the short-term end product and on assessment by comparison with adult models. There is also a widespread belief that children will learn only if adults tell them and that 'feeding' them the information in carefully sequenced steps is the best way to promote learning. However, it is far more natural for children to learn through experiences with art materials in an environment that encourages experimentation and where their responses are not judged as 'right' or 'wrong'.

In the approach to art teaching set out in this book, the emphasis is on 'process' rather than product. Children are encouraged to develop their understanding of ideas and feelings and to develop techniques through an active and purposeful use of art materials. As John Dewey comments in his book *Democracy and Education*, '. . . current theory about elementary art places as high a premium on the values of the learning "situation" [or process] as on its products.'[1]

Setting children the task of producing a piece of art using a prescribed technique does little to extend their experiences or ideas. The development of skills or techniques in art is, of course, important. However, these are best learned as the children struggle to express their ideas and should be related to the needs of the learner. The meaning or content of a piece is always of the utmost importance. Skills and techniques should therefore be regarded as means to ends rather than as things to be learned for themselves. As techniques are acquired, they should be practised by being put to use in other works that are under the personal control of the learner.

So how do you *teach* art without stifling individual creativity?

In an address to the PETA-ETA Conference in May 1983, Dr Brian Cambourne of the University of Wollongong identified seven conditions necessary for the effective learning of language. These conditions can also apply to the process of learning through art.

CONDITIONS FOR LEARNING

Immersion

Art holds a special appeal for children. From the moment they grasp an object and discover that it can make marks on a surface, or reshape a piece of modelling material, they quickly become immersed in the process and this makes effective learning easy.

In the classroom children should use the various art materials in workshop conditions as they are then free to experiment and take risks. The expression of ideas—the content of the piece—is the first priority. Artistic concepts and techniques are then developed through regular use.

Ultimately, children should learn through art. As well as being a vehicle of communication, art allows them to clarify their own thoughts, ideas and experiences. To enable this learning process to occur, children need to be exposed to a wide variety of materials and expressive activities. They also need many opportunities to discuss art and to see different styles and techniques.

Demonstration

Experiences involving artists at work are particularly valuable. Visit the studios of local artists and craftspeople, or invite them into the classroom, so that they can demonstrate the various aspects of their crafts. Elderly people can also be introduced to the art program in this way. Teachers can experiment with materials—and become aware of their possibilities or limitations—as they present them to the children.

Visits to factories, potteries, galleries and exhibitions help to make children aware of the complex processes involved in making a final product in any area of art.

Displays of children's work and the work of other artists provide many opportunities for discussion. Children should be encouraged to discover and evaluate the ideas and techniques in completed works.

Expectation

Creative ability is something which all children have; it is not a special talent that is reserved for a gifted minority. Learners at any stage in an art class have the ability to produce something that for them is new, superior or unique when compared with previous efforts.

Enthusiasm is very important for both teachers and students. Teachers should project the feeling that art is an enjoyable and valuable activity and that success is within the reach of everybody. These heightened expectations are then passed on to the learners and they respond accordingly. With success comes confidence as the children and teachers gain mastery over materials and techniques.

Approximation

'Imperfections' or 'misses' should really be called approximations. Approximations are an integral part of learning; they precede mastery over materials and the creative processes associated with these materials. The products of children's art work should always be viewed as stages in the process of learning to paint, draw, construct and so on. They should not be judged as inferior to adult art. There will inevitably be false starts, changes of direction, selection and rejection as children strive to refine and present an end product.

Practice/employment

Because of this emphasis on the processes involved in the expression of ideas, ample time and importance must be given to art within the primary school curriculum. Isolated 'one-off' experiences or lessons are no substitute for a process of development. Continuity of experience assists the learning process, strengthens understanding and improves the quality of the art work. As children's knowledge grows and they master new techniques, they should be given plenty of opportunities to employ these techniques.

Art, therefore, should not be seen as a separate and somewhat 'elitist' part of the curriculum, but as another tool for learning, an expression of individual thoughts and ideas on many different subjects. Art activities should be integrated with the various subject areas of the primary curriculum.

Responsibility

In traditional approaches to art learning children were often presented with set materials and tools and told in detail how to produce a piece designed by someone else. In this approach, however, control rests with the learner and the teacher's role is to provide guidance and support to permit a natural progression in the children's expression of ideas. Artists ought to have a great deal of freedom in the choice of both subject matter and manner of expression of ideas.

However, as Gaitskell and Hurwitz have observed, '. . . freedom in the art program does not mean unlimited licence. Teachers, in attempting to move children beyond a plateau of development, must constantly make certain decisions regarding their instructions. In so doing, however, they are always guided by the need for options — choices to be made by the individual child during the course of the art activity.'[2] For instance, in a painting entitled 'The Haunted House' teachers can present and discuss with the children various choices for content (ghosts, witches, bats, spider webs), colours (icy blues and greys, black, bright yellow, red) and methods of paint application (using a 'wash' to create mist, making sharp outlines with thick paint and a stick). It is then up to the children to decide which of these various ideas and techniques to use.

Tasks can also be presented in the form of problems to solve. Then, through the processes of trialling, accepting and rejecting, the children express their ideas at their own level and in their own way.

Children should be encouraged at a very early age to operate independently once having decided on a particular task. The main objective is always the completion of an important piece *to the artist's satisfaction*.

Feedback

At all stages of the process children should be encouraged to share responses — to discuss their work and the work of others with peers and adults. This feedback enables artists to modify and extend their ideas. They might as a result want to change their techniques, tools or materials. Positive responses lead to greater effort and self-criticism and to the further development of techniques.

Children's development in art comes both from inside themselves and from the world outside (this is, of course, true of development in any field of knowledge). They need to know about forms in nature and so on, and to be exposed to new ideas; at the same time they have to recast what they have experienced. As in any process of development, art learning involves the understanding of concepts which are then challenged or reinforced. It is a constant process of selection and rejection. In the process, children need to acquire an aesthetic sense, an ability to appreciate and judge art. This can best be developed in a congenial classroom environment where art is displayed and discussed.

Note: Many of the strategies and activities outlined in this program are adapted from techniques used by teachers in the area of language learning. To a certain extent, the teaching strategies used by Donald Graves in 'process writing' have been adapted to suit the area of art learning. The organisational ideas and ideas for classroom resources have also been adapted where applicable.

---

1 Dewey, *Democracy and Education*, p.5
2 Gaitskell and Hurwitz, *Children and Their Art*, p.28

A PATTERN OF GROWTH

Researchers and teachers have observed the development of children's art and discovered that there are clearly distinguishable stages. These stages have been documented by Linderman and Linderman in texts such as *Arts and Crafts for the Classroom*.

THE SCRIBBLING STAGE

The first stage of growth for young artists can be referred to as the Scribbling stage. Children begin with **Disorganized Scribbling**. When they start to control their movements with the crayon or other materials, they go on to

Controlled Scribbling. As the children gain further experience with the materials, they learn to vary the way in which they use them; the result is **Variable Scribbling**. The last, **Named Scribbling**, is significant because the children begin to 'name' the forms they put together. They begin to tell stories about what they are doing and give titles to particular pieces.

Children have already learnt a great deal about art, and have begun to experiment with it, before they arrive at school. The examples below, of the various phases of Scribbling, illustrate what children can discover for themselves from observing the world around them.

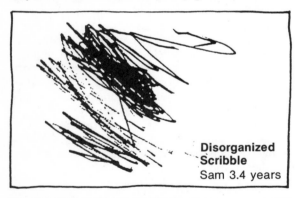

Disorganized Scribble
Sam 3.4 years

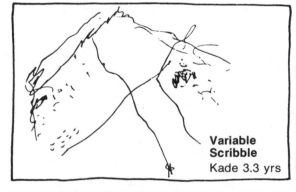

Variable Scribble
Kade 3.3 yrs

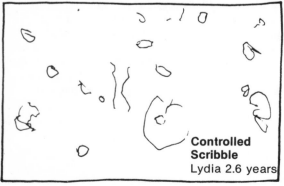

Controlled Scribble
Lydia 2.6 years

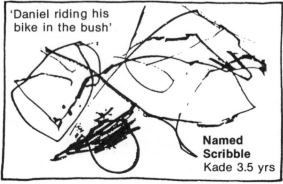

'Daniel riding his bike in the bush'

Named Scribble
Kade 3.5 yrs

Teachers should build on this early interest in painting, drawing, modelling and so on. The first lessons should focus on getting young children to experiment freely with art materials and to draw on knowledge which they already have about natural and man-made forms. Provide them with experiences whereby they will discover things through their senses.

Gradually they will move from the Scribbling stage to the first representations of objects such as figures, houses, trees and the like. The pieces below are Holly's first representations of a bear. Through experimentation in a natural learning environment, the representation has been refined over a period of time.

As at all stages in this program, it is important to give children repeated opportunities to model and to make marks. Encourage the children to talk about the ideas they have represented and to place value on their own efforts, just as adults are seen to value and appreciate works of art. When children are surrounded by art works, photographs, collections of beautiful or interesting things—and all their own attempts are encouraged—they will begin to value art.

There is no clearly defined border between the free experimentation with materials already outlined and the beginning of a structured program. When you consider that the children are ready to learn new techniques, create opportunities to introduce them. They can be presented gradually as an extension of techniques already learned; for instance, you could introduce them to the pinched method of hand-building with clay or to making simple objects for use in print-making.

THE PRIMARY STAGE

The next stage of development can be called the Primary Stage. Here the children see themselves as the dominant figure. There are no correct proportions and, in their art, the children include only those parts that are important or meaningful for them.

'A bear'
Holly 5.0 yrs

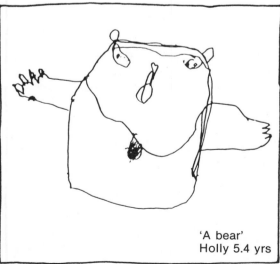

'A bear'
Holly 5.4 yrs

'My Dad'
Holly 5.6 yrs

'John'
Dylan 5.2 yrs

Bernadette 4.4 yrs

For children at this stage every experience is a new one. They like to play and pretend and use their imaginations. Teachers should therefore utilize various avenues to discovery; in particular, they should provide the children with experiences which will enable them to discover or perceive things through their senses.

Children at this stage like to arrive at forms for the objects they want to represent. For this reason provide simple subjects which have definite and easily learned outlines, such as people, houses and animals. The children's discoveries about how to represent things should be recorded and displayed on charts or in books. They can then be referred to and compared at other times.

As in the previous stage, children will initially have difficulty in learning the uses of tools and techniques. So provide guidance, as well as plenty of time for practice. When the materials are mastered, the ideas, the story, the message can be expressed.

Any completed piece needs to be treated with respect. Teachers need to learn how to receive both children's thoughts and the forms that reveal them. They need to show real interest by encouraging and praising all attempts, without bringing undue attention to the 'errors' that are a part of learning.

At this stage the children should also begin to discuss each other's work, and the work of artists from outside the classroom. These discussions should focus on both the subject matter and the way it is expressed, though initially more time should be devoted to the former. Good questioning of both the topic and the form leaves control with the children.

Questions such as,

Where is this?
What did you tell us about this part?

help the artists to focus on the meaning of the piece.

They can then be encouraged to expand on what they have said. For example,

Can you tell us more about this part?
Can you add anything here?
I don't quite understand this part. Can you explain it?

Some discussion of the form of the piece can follow as the children question the use of materials and techniques. For example,

How did you join this piece to that?
What did you use to make that mark?

Many ideas for questioning are given in the Developing Concepts and Techniques sections of this program.

6

THE INTERMEDIATE STAGE

This is the third stage. Children at this stage are moving out of their preoccupation with themselves; they are discovering that others are exciting to be with and to share ideas with. They are co-operative, willing to listen to opposing ideas and like to share in planning. They also like to develop ideas and to extend and refine techniques they have learnt.

This is the stage to encourage children to pay more attention to particular aspects of line, shape, patterns, texture and colour. Aspects of colour (such as strength and shade) and of line (such as thickness, length, direction and movement) should be highlighted. The children are also beginning to develop composing techniques. They pay attention to the arrangement of the objects on a page, draw and present objects in proportion, and balance one object against another. Alesha is experimenting by drawing things from different viewpoints.

The children are now ready for more involved sharing and discussion sessions. Discuss the various crafts and how artists use various media. Now is the time to bring guest artists into the classroom. Trips to artists' studios and galleries are also useful. Children can discuss their pieces with one another; they can talk about the ideas behind a piece, how the piece developed, and the techniques and methods used. This process of sharing for responses helps to provide new insights and to clarify ideas. Afterwards many children will naturally return to a piece to subtract or add parts, use a different method or technique, or even to reject the piece altogether and begin again.

Learning Experiences and sample questions to develop children's ideas at this stage are included in Phase 3 in each section of the program.

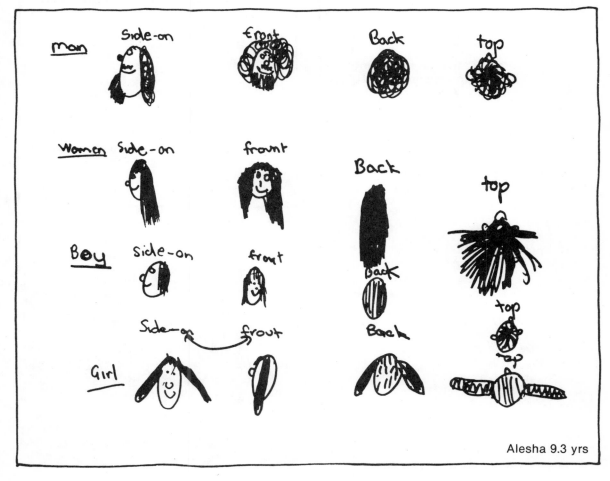

Alesha 9.3 yrs

THE UPPER INTERMEDIATE STAGE

The fourth stage may be termed Upper Intermediate. At this stage the children are being guided towards independence. They are becoming more critical of their own and others' efforts as they develop the ability to make judgements and decisions about content, methods and likely communicative effectiveness.

There is a maturing in the children's understanding of art. By now they have a working repertoire of techniques, ideas and art vocabulary and a foundation for analysing, discussing and appreciating various kinds of craft products. They like to work independently and for longer periods of time. Children pay greater attention to detail, often attempting to depict mirror reality, as is shown in the following sketches.

More involved techniques that emphasize the various aspects of design and composition can be introduced to children at this stage. Art concepts dealing with spatial visualization (such as perspective, vanishing distances and both realistic and abstract variations on space) can be developed with children.

Children at this stage need frequent opportunities to extend their techniques and concepts so they can make choices concerning the most effective means to communicate their ideas to others. It is important to emphasize originality in forming ideas and working with art media. The children also need to give and develop reasons for the aesthetic choices they make so they can analyse, appreciate and make judgements concerning their own and others' efforts. Ideas for the development of techniques and sample questions to guide the children to become self-critical are provided in Phase 4 of each area of the program.

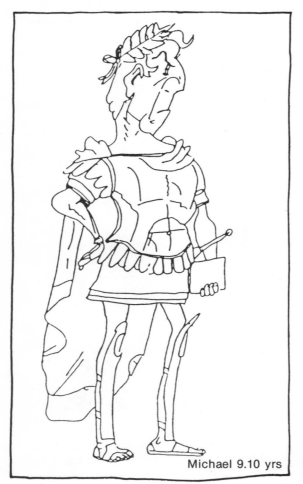

Michael 9.10 yrs

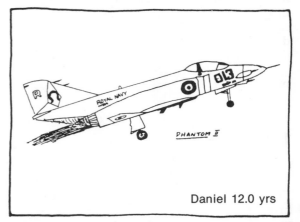

Daniel 12.0 yrs

Greg 12.4 yrs

THE PROGRAM STRUCTURE

This program has been developed to answer the following questions:
- How does one learn to create, experience and understand art?
- What is the teacher to do in the classroom to facilitate this learning?
- How can a program for art be effectively planned?

The purpose of the program is to provide teachers with a practical framework to guide them in structuring the learning experiences through which children can discover and develop satisfying techniques of expression through art.

There are three structures within the program.

1. THE PROGRAM IN SIX AREAS

First, the program has been divided into six broad areas, namely Painting, Drawing, Clay-modelling, Print-making, Textiles, and Construction.

In each of these areas the program presents Learning Objectives and sample Learning Experiences to enable teachers to plan effectively.

2. THE LEARNING OBJECTIVES IN FOUR PHASES

Within each subject area the Learning Objectives have been divided into four groups, called Phases. The Phases correspond to these natural stages of development:

- beginning experiences with art, and developing basic ideas and techniques (Phases 1 and 2)
- modifying and extending ideas and techniques (Phase 3)
- refining ideas and techniques (Phase 4).

The stages of development in children's art are well researched and documented. The previous chapter, 'A Pattern of Growth', briefly outlines the process of development which has been used in this program to assign appropriate Learning Objectives and Learning Experiences to the four Phases.

It must be noted, however, that the program is based on the beliefs that artistic learning is not an automatic consequence of maturation and that learning can be facilitated through sensitive intervention and guidance. Any reference to phases based on ages, years of schooling or grades is carefully avoided. The Phases in the program have been devised for practical reasons to enable teachers to make their own decisions about appropriate learning experiences for their children. The development of artistic techniques is seen as an intensely personal and individual matter that is not defined by artificial and rigid groupings, but by the children's ability to respond to and benefit from their own experiences with art.

3. THE LEARNING EXPERIENCES IN THREE STAGES

The third structure applies to the Learning Experiences. These have been divided into three Stages: Getting Started, Developing Concepts and Techniques, and Crafting and Presenting. The activities associated with each Stage are:

Getting Started

- Introduction to materials
- Discussion and rehearsal of ideas and techniques
- Decision to use materials and techniques
- Searching for additional information and ideas

Developing Concepts and Techniques

- Attempting and experimenting with ideas and techniques
- Revising and modifying ideas and techniques following audience response through discussion
- Refining and polishing ideas and techniques

Crafting and Presenting

- Choosing the form to suit a piece
- Presenting and displaying a piece to an audience for a response to the completed work

Teachers should plan their sessions by selecting appropriate Learning Experiences from some or each of these Stages.

TEACHING STRATEGIES

DISCUSSION

One of the most valuable experiences for learning artists is the simple but powerful interaction which occurs between them and those around them. Children should discuss their own and other artists' work at different stages in the process. The most valuable teaching strategy, therefore, is the use of intermittent meetings between the child (artist) and the teacher and peers (audience) as a piece develops.

Discussion, or sharing for responses, can be guided by purposeful questioning. The questions lead children to look closely at the work of other artists and to make judgements about the ideas presented and the medium and techniques used. They can then make similar observations about their own work.

Questions may first focus on the subject matter of a piece, and its expressive or artistic qualities. Include questions such as:

What is the artist trying to tell us?

Is there a story here?
What is it?
Is this a realistic story?
How does this work of art make you feel?
What does it make you think of?
Do you like it?
Why do you like it?
How is the medium used?
What effects are created?
How is it composed?
Is the work organized?
How can you see that it is organized?

Discussion may then focus on specific techniques with questions such as:

What medium has the artist used?
What techniques might the artist have used?
How did the artist create these marks?
What tool(s) could the artist have used to form the piece?
Can you use similar techniques to create these effects?

Some questions may also be evaluative and lead children to make judgements about art such as:

Does the work tell you where the artist lived?
Does the artist express his/her understanding in a unique manner?
How is this piece different from others you have seen?
How can this piece compare with others by the same artist/by other artists?
What is the artist trying to say in this work?
Does the artist suggest new ways of seeing things?
What makes a work of art great?
What makes an artist great?

Both teachers and children need a growing bank of terms in each area of the program for use in these discussions. These words can be introduced gradually and within the context of the children's experiences with the medium. Examples are included in the Learning Objectives sections for each Phase.

There should always be a degree of humour and light-heartedness in the discussions. The atmosphere should be relaxed, enabling children to speak openly and freely about their efforts, knowing that they will receive support and guidance.

ORGANIZATION

Set routines enable this interaction to function smoothly and efficiently. Art sessions should follow predictable sequences so that questioning techniques become familiar to children. In this program, sample questions are provided at various stages in the process to enable teachers to establish these routines and questioning patterns. The range of questions is limited to draw attention to only a few features of a piece. In addition, the focus for questioning in each Phase is initially on content and ideas, followed by means of expression and techniques.

Because the sequence of these discussions is predictable, they allow for reversible role relationships where the artist can ask the audience to respond to the content of a piece and the techniques used. The audience can then make suggestions—perhaps in the form of solutions to problems or alternatives for consideration. Having received this feedback, the child can select the most appropriate path to follow.

Discussions can occur between teacher and child, child and another child or group of children depending on the organizational aspects of the classroom. Ideally, classroom areas should be provided to promote informal discussion between artists and audience.

The structures and the management of time in the sessions can be decided by each school or individual teacher depending on the resources available.

ENVIRONMENT

The surroundings in which art takes place can provide inspiration, encouragement and a sense of satisfaction and pride. The environment can provide opportunities for building vocabularies, stretching imaginations, clarifying meaning, strengthening techniques and fostering enthusiasm for art.

Part of the art room or classroom can be set aside for the display of published works as well as ideas for young artists. In this area you could:

- develop a classroom centre where children can bring in any object that they consider beautiful and want to share
- provide an exhibit space where original work can be attractively displayed. Local galleries or private collectors can often lend examples. You could also exchange exhibits with other grades or with other schools
- compile a class catalogue of the children's exhibits
- make a tape recording of the children's descriptions of their exhibits to accompany the display
- start a file collection of examples of beautiful and interesting things for the children to add to. Provide magazines and newspapers for cutting out. Trade something each week with another class
- make charts or mobiles displaying terms, methods, topic ideas, descriptions of processes and sample discussion questions
- compile word lists on themes or topics such as 'Colour', 'Shape', 'Texture', 'Movement', 'Line' and so on
- start a collection of art books, catalogues, slides or photographs for the children to browse through for ideas
- begin a class set of art learning books or charts where the children can record discoveries in categories such as: famous artists, functional art, decorative art, Australian art, techniques in art, art tools and materials
- record children's responses or judgements about art works on charts or a class graffiti board.

I don't like the colours.

There's lots of detail; it must have taken ages.

It's not useful.

I don't like the sculpture because it doesn't look real.

The picture makes me feel bright and happy.

EVALUATION

It is the children's task to react to their own artistic works and to other children's pieces. As they criticize and refine their own pieces, they are conducting self-evaluation. A child's concept of what is good in art comes through exposure to models and to other children's pieces and from the reactions of others to his or her own pieces.

The teacher can help this process of awareness by:
- being close by and supportive as the children develop their ideas and techniques
- asking questions, drawing attention to certain specific points, and providing directions
- giving a pattern.

Basically the teacher's role is to help the artist to develop the best work possible. As a piece of art evolves help the student to identify his or her strengths and to build on these strengths. It is much better to give advice while a piece is in an unfinished form. When the work is finished, do not 'mark' it or otherwise place an assessment on it. Assessment takes away the artist's ownership and sense of responsibility for his or her own work.

The art should be judged only in relation to the artist's satisfaction with his or her own work and in relation to its communicative effectiveness. Audience response is an indication of the latter.

The teacher should:
- help children to evaluate their own efforts by challenging them

  Is this as good as your last piece?
  Is there any way you can improve this piece?

- build confidence and not dwell on imperfections. As confidence grows, the children become more involved in self-evaluation
- avoid giving false praise. Refrain from making general praising statements such as, 'Oh that's great', 'Fine, it's wonderful', when both the teacher and the child know that there are some points that need improvement
- never take the ownership of a piece away from the artist and proceed to 'fix up' last-minute details

- avoid judgements and comments that could make the artist feel that the teacher's reaction is the only one that matters. Avoid evaluative comments such as 'A good painting', 'Good work'.

The young artists should be guided towards a process of continuous self-questioning.

What will this piece be about?
Who is going to view/use this piece?
Is this the best way to start?
Where can I go from here?
In what other way can I develop this piece?
Which part of my piece shows the most promise?
What is the focus/most important part of the piece?
How can I improve it?
What do I need to work on?
What's good in this piece?
Is my piece expressive/beautiful/useful?
Did the audience understand it and enjoy it?
How does it compare with my other pieces?

As the children develop as independent artists, they should be given more responsibility for self-evaluation. This can be done in various ways. You could:
- ask the children to rate their pieces and to give reasons for their ratings
- ask the children to look back over past pieces and rank them, again giving reasons
- ask the children to write a report. These reports could begin 'I have recently learnt a number of things about drawing . . .' or 'My painting has improved because . . .'

Keeping evaluation records

There are many evaluation techniques, but some demand more time than a teacher can possibly give. The following techniques are particularly suitable for the evaluation of art.
- Keep a 'profile' or 'log' as a type of informal assessment.
- During or following sessions make jottings which record children's strengths and weaknesses or mastery of techniques.
- Keep records of small group discussions.
- Keep work samples in an artist's folio. In particular, select pieces which record periodic developments in an area (painting, drawing and so on) of the art program.

Artist's folders

Fold

PIECE COMPLETED	DATE
1. Coil Pot	25·2·86
2. Paper Monster	4·4·86
3. Spring Painting	19·4·86
4. Sports Drawing	10.7.86
5. Clay Model	11.8.86
6. Papier Mâché	18.9.86
7.	
8.	
9.	
10.	
11.	
12.	
13.	

My
Art
Folder

Marcus Laurie
Grade 4.

TOPICS	MARCUS KNOWS
① Our farm	① How to make clay coils
② My dentist trip	② How to paint a background
③ My dog Bootsie	③ How to draw moving people
④ Fishing	④ How to glue and tape cardboard and paper
⑤ When I went to the snow	

Fold

Older children may keep an artist's folder as a record of their efforts during the process of development. It contains three main sections.

1 'Ideas to begin with' or 'Topics'
The child lists possible ideas or topics. Not all of these will be attempted. The teacher can refer to this section to see if the child needs help in expressing his or her ideas.

2 'Things I can do' or 'Things I know about'
The child or teacher compiles a list of the techniques that the child has demonstrated in his or her work.

3 'Pieces I have completed'
The child lists pieces completed and the date of completion.

Display Cards

THINGS WE KNOW ABOUT – PAPIER MÂCHÉ

- To tear the paper from the fold down.
- To keep pieces light so they can hang.
- To attach pieces with tape or string before using paste.
- To use plain paper for the last coat.
- To let the last coat dry well so the paint doesn't crack.
- To add some glue to the paint so it doesn't crack.

Through questions asked, the teacher is constantly assessing how each artist is progressing with his or her piece. These questions ultimately assist children to ask similar questions for themselves at different stages during the process. Points of interest or points that need clarification may be recorded during the discussion on display cards. These are also a record of the children's understandings at a particular time and may be positioned around the room for future reference. Since children are involved in the compilation of these charts, it is important that the wording be, as far as possible, their own. That is, the charts should make sense to them.

Class display

The children can contribute their best piece of art every fortnight or month to a class display. This serves as an evaluation record and can also be used by other classes for art judgement sessions.

Learning Objectives checklist

A checklist can be drawn up from the desired Learning Objectives for each area. This serves as a record of each child's development and can be a valuable aid to further program planning.

Sample: PAINTING

Phase 1 1. Can match, sort and mix colours. 2. Uses a variety of paints. 3. Can apply paint using brushes. 4. Can select a topic/idea. 5. Discusses efforts with others. 6. Uses appropriate painting terms.						
Phase 2 1. Can match, sort, classify and mix colours. 2. Identifies primary colours. 3. Mixes secondary colours. 4. Uses a variety of paints and brushes. 5. Uses implements other than brushes. 6. Knows methods of care of equipment. 7. Uses appropriate painting terms.						
Phase 3 1. Can match, sort, classify and mix colours to achieve specific effects. 2. Mixes colours to solve problems. 3. Uses colours to express mood. 4. Uses a variety of painting techniques and materials. 5. Can apply paint to various surfaces. 6. Spends time refining and polishing a painting. 7. Uses appropriate painting terms.						
Phase 4 1. Uses colour for a variety of purposes. 2. Selects appropriate techniques and styles to suit a purpose. 3. Spends time to plan, develop, complete and present a painting. 4. Uses appropriate painting terms.						

PAINTING
Phase 1

LEARNING OBJECTIVES

1 Children will be introduced to and explore the idea of colour through matching, sorting and mixing.
2 Children will be introduced to paint and discover what paint can do.
3 Children will learn the techniques of applying paint using brushes.
4 Children will be able to make decisions about the subject and content of their pieces.
5 Children will discuss the idea of 'a painting' and value their own and others' efforts.
6 Children will become familiar with language relating to painting: primary colours (red, blue, yellow), brushes (round, soft, hard, flat, short, long, dabbing, rolling, twisting, twirling, dripping), paint (thick, thin, smooth, rough, dry, wet, powder), artist, painting, gallery.

LEARNING EXPERIENCES

Getting Started

Introduce and explore colour
Blow bubbles, on a sunny day if possible, and let the children see the spectrum (rainbow) colours in them. Or make a rainbow by turning your back to the sun and turning on a hose with a sprinkler attachment.

Look at the colour sequence: red, orange, yellow, green, blue, indigo, violet.

Visit colourful places
Take your class to a pet shop which sells tropical fish or colourful birds to see the variety of colours.

Record the children's reactions:

One fish had red fins.
There was a fish which had yellow and black stripes.
The budgies were light blue and light green.
The orange fish had long tails.

Make coloured glasses
Make spectacles out of card and cover the frames with coloured cellophane. Children can see how the colours of objects change through the coloured glasses.

Explore the use of paint
Provide the children with a variety of paint types and allow them to explore the potential of each by using a brush. For example, they could try mixed powder paint on bulky newsprint, finger paint on litho paper (one colour), acrylic or poster paint on bulky newsprint.

Encourage the children to relate their experiences to each other by letting them work in small groups.

Record the children's efforts on sheets of paper or on the chalkboard. You could also make charts like the ones which follow.

WHAT I CAN DO WITH PAINT-
dab
write
slop
STREAK
drip
draw

PAINT CAN BE —

- thick
- thin
- smooth
- rough
- runny
- dry
- gooey
- slippery
- slimy
- flaky

Experiment with brushes

Provide the children with a variety of brushes (soft, hard, flat, thick, thin, round, short bristle, long bristle) and acrylic paint (primary colours: red, yellow, blue). Encourage the children to experiment with brushes — by rolling, swirling, twisting, dabbing, moving slowly, moving fast — to create a variety of shapes, lines and colours.

Record the children's efforts. Make charts like the one below.

WHAT WE CAN DO WITH BRUSHES —

- a red line by rolling
- a blue swirl
- a green shape by twisting
- yellow dabs
- drips of black
- purple streaks
- splashes of orange
- loops of brown

Developing Concepts and Techniques

The children's personal experiences are the main source of ideas for beginning artists. Ideas may also be generated through drama, stories, poems and class outings, or through class or group discussions or brain-storming sessions.

Discussion questions help children to clarify their ideas.

What things can you do?
What do you know about . . . ?
What is an artist?
Where do we go to look at paintings?
What is a painting?
Why do we paint?
What do you like to paint?

Compile and display lists of topics for children to use: My Dad, At the Beach, Toys, My Dog, Riding My Bike.

For very young children who are just learning how to apply paint, the 'painting' is completed quickly. The first effort is the finished product. The children's techniques can be developed systematically to enable them to focus on ideas. The following activities are useful in developing techniques.

Paint and brush activities

Using a thick brush and green paint, paint a curved shape.

Using a thin brush and red paint, paint a long twisted line.

Using a thick brush, paint swirls of your favourite colour.

Using any brush, dab many colours on your paper.

Colour-matching activities

Paint using the colour of: the sky, a rosy apple, the grass, the curtains, your car, your clothes.

Colour-mixing activities

Using primary colours, paint and find the new colour(s).

Dab one colour on to the paper and dab another on to it. Find the new colour.

Paint one colour and paint another over the top. Find the new colour.

Finger paint with one colour then another. Find the new colours.

Finger paint with three primary colours. Find the new colour.

Discussion

Encourage the children to discuss their 'paintings' with peers at various stages during the process. The discussions will naturally focus on the ideas, the content of a piece.

During the sharing time, the following questions may begin the discussion.

Tell me (us) about your picture.

Does your painting have a name?

What is this part?

Then focus more closely on the content with questions from either peers or the teacher.

When did you do this?

What else did you do there?

Which part do you like?

Which is the most important part?

What is this part?

Could you explain what this bit is?

Techniques may also be discussed.

Did you make any new colours?

How?

Do you know the names of these new colours?

How did you use the brush to make this mark?

Did you use all the colours?

Is this thick or thin paint?

Crafting and Presenting

Here are some ideas for the kinds of paintings that can be completed and displayed in this Phase.

The children could paint:
- using fingers and primary colours
- to illustrate stories, poems and shared experiences such as a class excursion
- pictures in a sequence to illustrate an event, outing or story
- using specified techniques; for example, a pattern of 'swirls' and 'dabs', by twisting and curling lines of paint
- to enhance a model during construction activities; for example, masks, puppets.

PAINTING
Phase 2

LEARNING OBJECTIVES

1 Children will explore the variety of colour (shades, intensity) through matching, sorting, classifying and mixing.
2 Children will identify primary colours and mix them to create secondary colours.
3 Children will make use of a variety of paints and brushes for different purposes.
4 Children will explore the methods of applying paint using implements other than brushes.
5 Children will learn how to care for paints and implements.
6 Children will produce a piece that can be shared and discussed with others.
7 Children will become familiar with language relating to painting: secondary colours (pink, grey, green, purple, orange), colour wheel, colour matching, colour mixing, palette.

LEARNING EXPERIENCES

Getting Started

Match colours

Children can match colours in objects that are all around them: flowers, objects and furniture in the classroom, the clothes they wear.

Find an object that is the same colour as your jumper.

Find other objects that are the same colour as the chairs in the room.

Sort colours

Use beads, buttons, counters and pieces of wool or fabric, and sort them according to colour. Children can string the beads into simple graded patterns.

Picture story books

Browse through picture story books with the children and discuss the variety of colours used in the illustrations. Encourage the children to name and describe the colours.

Look at photographs

Show slides or photographs of colourful scenes and let the children discuss what they see. Try to include photos of signs from the environment and other objects that rely on colour for their effect.

Make colourful collections

Examine collections of as many objects as possible of the same colour (various shades) and discuss these through questions such as:

Are the objects the same colour?

How are they the same?

How are they different?

Which is your favourite?

The objects can be sorted according to colour.

Experiment with dyes

Add dyes to jars of water or to wet cartridge paper and discover the variety of colours created.

Experiment with paints and brushes

Discover how brushes can be used to apply paint — by rolling, twisting, swirling, dabbing, spattering, dripping.

Discover how different-sized brushes can be used — to draw thin lines, to fill in large areas, to apply paint thickly/thinly.

Discuss why we use different brushes and paint — thick brushes for large areas, thin brushes for detail; thick paint to make details stand out, thin paint to cover a large area.

Use other implements

Experiment with applying paint using a variety of implements other than brushes. You could use man-made tools (string, straws, pieces of cardboard, crumpled paper, sponges, rollers, ice-cream sticks) or natural tools (twigs, leaves, sticks, feathers).

Developing Concepts and Techniques

These activities help children to express their ideas with more confidence.

Colour-mixing activities

Using the three primary colours and white, the children discover how many colours they can mix.

Each new discovery can be recorded on a chart with the artist's name underneath.

Make a colour wheel using the three primary colours to mix the three secondary colours.

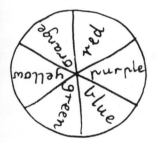

red and blue = purple
yellow and red = orange
yellow and blue = green

Ask the children to identify the primary colours (red, blue, yellow). Then demonstrate the method of mixing colours, using a mixing board or palette.

Paint application activities

Apply paint with a brush by dabbing, ('stipple') rolling, twisting, stroking and so on.

Apply thick and thin paint by stippling thick paint, stroking ('washing') thin paint, rolling and twisting thick paint, dribbling and dripping thin paint.

To highlight certain techniques, set specific tasks for the children.

Stipple with red paint, wash your brush and stipple with the yellow. Try to create a new colour as the colours blend. What is the new colour?

Paint your section of paper using a wash of blue, now stipple over in one spot using thick yellow paint. Can you see a new colour?

Discussion

As in Phase 1, discussion should concentrate initially on ideas (the content of the painting) and may then extend to focus on techniques. Children need direction in order to give effective responses.

Tell the artist what's good about the painting.

Tell the artist what's best in the painting

Sharing time can proceed through questions such as:

What is your painting about?

Tell us about this part?

I don't quite understand this part; can you explain it to me?

Could you change any part of this painting?

Is there anything you could add?

Children may embark on another piece as a result of these discussions which allow them to clarify and refine their ideas.

Try revising a painting by changing or adding things in a small group or as a class.

Techniques can also be highlighted through discussion.

Which brushes did you use?

What technique did you use to make this mark?

Are there any colours in your painting which are not in the palette?

Do you know the names of these new colours?

Can you remember how you made this colour?

Refer to the colour wheel to locate the 'new' colours the children discover. -

Crafting and Presenting

The children could paint:

• using primary colours and white (children's choice of topic)
• to illustrate their own writing as big books, charts or posters
• a mural as a small-group activity
• by applying paint with implements other than brushes; for example, by blowing with a straw, by using crumpled paper and pieces of cardboard
• using specified techniques; for example, rolling, twisting, stippling, 'washing'
• to enhance a model during construction activities.

PAINTING
Phase 3

LEARNING OBJECTIVES

1 Children will match, sort and mix colours to achieve different effects (in shade, tone, intensity, appeal).
2 Children will use their techniques of mixing colours and apply them to problem-solving situations.
3 Children will explore the use of colour to express a mood or a feeling in a painting.
4 Children will use a variety of techniques and implements to apply paint for specific purposes.
5 Children will apply paint to a variety of surfaces.
6 Children will gain confidence in the use of techniques and concepts and show a willingness to discuss their uses.
7 Children will work a painting, refine it and present it to an audience.
8 Children will become familiar with language relating to painting: palette knife, application, tone, tint, strong, pale, light, bright, dark, vivid, bold, rich, warm colours, cool colours, colour contrast, natural, man-made, natural surfaces (bark, stones, rocks, sticks, wood), man-made surfaces (bulky news, litho, cardboard, plastic, fabric, hessian), print, landscape, moods and feelings, focus, foreground, background.

LEARNING EXPERIENCES

Getting Started

Discuss painting
Use a display of paintings or prints to stimulate interest and discussion through questions such as:

Do you like to paint?
How do you feel when you paint?
How do you feel when you look at paintings?
Where do you go to look at paintings?
Can everybody paint?
Are all paintings beautiful?
Do you like some paintings and dislike others?
Can you remember a painting you really liked/disliked?
What do you like to paint?

Learn about other artists
Visit a gallery to view exhibits. Invite an artist to display his or her works and talk to the children.

Discuss shades of colour
Look at colour charts (paint colour-cards, fabric or wallpaper samples) which show many shades of colours, and let the children describe them in their own words.

This is lighter than that.
These are brighter than those.
This is a dark colour compared to these.

Look at different tones or shades of the same colour; for example 'blue': sky blue, ink blue, cornflower blue, smokey blue, sea blue, etc. The children can produce some of these shades with their paints and find words to describe them.

Collect and sort colours
See how many small scraps of cloth of the same colour you can find. These can be sorted and arranged according to shade from 'strongest' to 'palest'. Pieces of coloured paper torn from magazines can also be sorted.

Describe colours

Look at contrasting colours and record the words children use to describe colours on cards, charts or in books.

DESCRIBE CONTRASTING COLOURS –
- light
- dark
- pale
- weak
- shade
- vivid
- bright
- strong
- bold
- rich
- match

Colours in nature

Look at colours in the environment and nature, and see how the shades and tones change with the seasons. You could make a colour wheel showing the colours most evident in each season, or set up a colour table of natural objects and change it as each season comes and goes.

Colours around the world

Look at slides or photographs of scenes around the world. Discuss, compare and contrast the colours. For example, compare the reds and browns of Australian landscapes with the greens and yellows of English and European landscapes.

Experiment with paints, brushes and surfaces

Keep on using a variety of paints and brushes and other implements for application (see page 20).

Explore other surfaces to paint on. You could use man-made surfaces (dry and wet paper, corrugated cardboard, fabric, glass, plastic, hessian, foam, tin, leather) or natural surfaces (bark, stones, rocks, sticks, wood).

Developing Concepts and Techniques

As children become proficient with materials and techniques, they will draw on their own artistic experience to expand their ideas and extend the content of their paintings. They will be more eager to experiment during the painting process. The teacher should present ideas and activities to encourage this development.

Use colour to express moods and feelings

Look at paintings and discuss how the artists have used colour to display a mood or a feeling; for example, heat, anger, serenity.

Discuss how certain colours make us feel.
red = anger, danger
yellow = joy, happiness
black = fear, death
blue = coolness, calmness
green = peace

Use questioning or group discussion to encourage children to suit their choice of colour to the content of a painting.

What are moods or feelings?

Choose a topic/idea that relates to a mood or feeling.

Does it have a title?

What colours might you use?

When others look at your painting how do you think they will feel?

Are you going to use more of certain colours to help you express your ideas?

Use colour to highlight a focal point

Look at paintings and discuss how the artists have used colour to highlight important parts.

Discuss the use of contrasting colours and bold colours as they are used in signs and posters.

Do certain colours catch your eye on a sign or poster?

Are there contrasting colours on the poster?

In advertising signs, posters or billboards, how important are the colours?

Which colours are best used near each other?

Use paint for different purposes

Apply a thin wash of paint as the background and then apply thicker paint to bring up the foreground.

Use blues and greys to create shadows in a painting.

Draw a picture using a dark crayon or pastel and apply a wash of colour to create a 'see-through' effect.

Use a variety of implements to apply paint

Experiment and discover how paint can be applied for different purposes.

Use thick paint applied with a palette knife to highlight the foreground.

Use thick paint with implements such as a comb, roller or corrugated card to create special effects and marks.

Use your hand or finger to smooth the paint and create a soft edge.

Apply texture prior to painting (sand, bark, twigs, etc.).

Discussion

Encourage the children to discuss the various methods of applying paint and the various uses of colour through questions such as:

What is your painting about?

Does it have a title?

Can you tell us more about this part?

What is the focal point/most important part of your painting?

Did you use a special technique or colour to highlight this part?

How do you think the audience will feel when they look at your painting?

Did you use any techniques or colours to show this?

Crafting and Presenting

The children could paint:
- using primary and secondary colours (children's choice of topic)
- using colours to express moods and feelings
- using contrasting colours
- to illustrate ideas in other subject areas; for example, Social Studies, Science, Language
- using a particular colour theme; for example, an Australian landscape
- by applying paint with implements other than brushes
- on a variety of surfaces; for example, bark, stones, sticks, wood.

PAINTING
Phase 4

LEARNING OBJECTIVES

1 Children will review and refine concepts relating to colour.
2 Children will use colour for a specific purpose in a painting.
3 Children will make wide use of the techniques of applying paint to various surfaces.
4 Children will select the most suitable techniques, colours or style to use in a painting.
5 Children will plan, develop and complete a painting and present it to an audience.
6 Children will become familiar with language relating to painting: implement, beautiful, expressive, technique, style, exhibits, exhibition, perspective, depth, decoration, fashion, advertisement, colour combinations, balance, textural painting, abstract, Expressionist, Symbolist, Impressionist.

LEARNING EXPERIENCES

Getting Started

Discuss individual paintings
Use a display of paintings or prints to stimulate interest and discussion and to highlight the artist's use of colour and methods of paint application through questions such as:

What is this painting about?/What does this painting tell you?
How do you feel when you look at the painting?
Has the artist used certain colours to express this feeling?
Is there a focus in the picture?

How has the artist displayed this?
How has the artist applied the paint?
Has the artist used implements other than brushes?

Discuss art generally
Discuss the range of visual arts—such as architecture (the art of building), the design of items produced by craftsmen or in a factory, sculpture (the art of making statues), and the art of making pictures (by drawing, painting, collage or printing)—through questions such as:

What good is art?
What is good art?
Is it beautiful?
Is it expressive?
Is it useful?
Is it any of these in combination?
What makes good art?
Is it the time it took to make an article?
Is it the material used?
Is it the artists' sensitivity and imagination or their techniques?
Is it the ideas or the message shown?

Look at the works of well-known artists
Using prints, slides and films, discuss the techniques used by well-known artists such as Van Gogh, Rembrandt, Leonardo Da Vinci.
Look at Australian artists from colonial days to the present.
Visit an art gallery to view exhibitions.

Talk to painters
Invite an artist to paint with and for the children. The children need to realize that painting is often not a 'one-off' event.

Use a view finder

Make a view finder to give the children an artist's 'view' of a scene. (Coloured cellophane may be inserted so that the children can see the world through a new colour.) Use the view finder to focus on areas of landscape, street scenes and so on.

Look at the idea of perspective

Have the children look at their surroundings to distinguish between background, middleground and foreground. Look at paintings also and pinpoint these three areas. Through these paintings the children may observe that colour and methods of paint application are used to create perspective (depth), as well as size relationships.

Look at the ways we use colour and paint

List them:
>   house paint — decoration
>   fabric dye — fashion
>   signs — advertising, conveying information
Look at the effects of various colours.
Direct the children's attention through questions such as:

> Can some colours on walls or posters be seen from greater distances than others?

> Which are the most popular colours for cars?

> What are the most fashionable colours for male/female clothing?

> Discuss pleasing colour combinations.
> Look at the things that can change a colour; for example, the effects of sunlight, weather and fire, the effect of bleach.

Developing Concepts and Techniques

Children in this Phase should be guided towards independence. They are becoming more critical of their own and others' efforts and more and more capable of making artistic judgements and decisions about content and techniques. The Getting Started section outlines many ideas and experiences which the following activities build upon.

Use perspective in a painting

Use a wash of paint in the background and gradually build up the paint to become thicker and more brilliant in the foreground.

Use blue to create a hazy effect in the background. (The hazy blue effect can be easily seen if you take the children outside to look at distant hills.)

Try to imitate particular styles of painting

Use the styles of artists such as Van Gogh, Picasso, Rembrandt and Cézanne.
Use the 'Impressionist' style of painting using 'dabs' or 'splashes' of primary colours.
Use the styles and colours of Australian artists.
Use the styles of non-realist artists, those who change the natural appearance of things in their pictures; for example, abstract, Expressionist and Symbolist artists.

Use colour for different purposes

Use colour: to express a mood or feeling; to show perspective; to create pleasing colour combinations and a balanced composition; to create a focus in a piece.

Use paint for different purposes

Use paint: to create texture with the use of a brush, stick, sponge or roller; to show perspective; to express a mood or feeling (for example, a thin wash for a peaceful mood or thick splashes for a more aggressive piece).

Discussion

Discussion before, during or after painting should centre around ideas and then extend to techniques.

> What is your piece telling us?
> Is there a focus to your piece?
> How did you create this focus?
> How will (does) the audience feel when they look at your painting?
> Did you use particular colours to express your ideas?
> Show us your palette; are there pleasing colour combinations?
> Did you use a particular style?
> Did you deliberately set out to create a special effect (perspective, texture, a mood or feeling)?
> What implements did you use to apply the paint?
> How did you apply it?

Crafting and Presenting

The children could paint:

- using a variety of colours for particular purposes; for example, to express moods and feelings, to show perspective
- from life sources; for example, a landscape
- using a particular style; for example, Impressionism, Surrealism
- a still life
- using a particular technique; for example, a 'wash'
- after deliberately applying texture
- a poster or billboard as an advertisement
- to illustrate ideas across subject areas; for example, in Social Studies, Science, Language
- to enhance a model during construction activities.

CLAY-MODELLING
Phase 1

LEARNING OBJECTIVES

1 Children will discover what clay can do and share their experiences with others.
2 Children will be able to make decisions about the subject and content of their pieces.
3 Children will value their efforts and the efforts of others.
4 Children will learn simple techniques of hand-building including the additive, subtractive, pinch and slab methods.
5 Children will create texture with a variety of natural and man-made materials.
6 Children will become familiar with language relating to clay: soft, smooth, cool, sticky, dry, bumpy, rough, flat, shape, push, pull, squeeze, roll, twist, add, subtract, slab, pinch, squeeze, scratch.

LEARNING EXPERIENCES

Getting Started

Introduce clay

Find and examine some clay in nature.
Explore clay through the senses and encourage the children's reactions to the feel, look and smell of clay. Record these responses.

It's cold and hard.
We can squash, squeeze, twist and curl it.
We can pound and punch it.

Compile a word list from the children's responses: cold, slushy, dry, gooey, slimy, wet, smooth, slippery, lumpy.

Look at the properties of clay

Use balls of clay and look at how clay changes: when we add water, when we make it warm with our hands and squeeze it, when it dries on our hands.

Look at how we can change the shape of the clay — by pulling, twisting, poking, scraping, cutting, tearing, rolling, pinching.

Make charts like the ones below.

Squeeze clay

Make a clay 'squeeze' by holding a ball of clay in one hand and squeezing it in different ways. In small groups discuss the shapes produced.

What does it look like?

Can you name it?

How can you change its shape to look like something else?

In pairs the children can act out a clay 'squeeze'. One child can pretend to mould the clay as the other gradually takes shape.

Developing Concepts and Techniques

For beginners who are struggling with the techniques of manipulating clay, the initial effort is often the finished product. The children may not want to change or develop a piece. The following activities build on the children's early experiences with modelling materials and develop manipulative techniques.

Make shapes

Make a shape that is: long, tall, round, flat, rough, smooth, curled, straight.

Make an object or shape by pulling out from a piece of clay without breaking anything off.

Break off or pull out pieces of clay to make a shape.

Use specific modelling methods

Make shapes or objects using the additive, substractive, pinch or slab methods.

Additive method

Build up the clay by adding simple shapes.

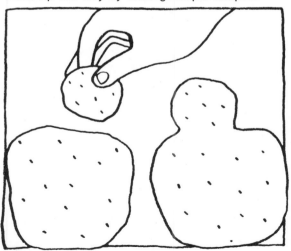

Subtractive method

Start with a large piece of clay, then pull pieces off to create a shape.

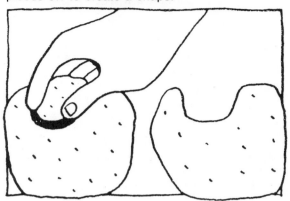

Pinch method

Roll a hand-sized ball of clay between the palms. Push down the centre of the ball with both (or one) thumb(s). Slowly force the thumbs out and begin to deepen and enlarge the hole you've made.
Gently pinch and rotate the ball to build out an even wall of clay.
Create and smooth your interesting shapes.

Slab method

On a flat surface, roll or pound out the clay until it is an even thickness (about 1 cm).
Cut, pull out or break away pieces to make a shape or object.

Use texture tools

Make a shape using the various methods introduced and use texture tools to decorate and enhance the piece. The tools may include: nails, sticks, stones, fingers, fingernails, buttons, gum nuts.

Record the words children use: lumpy, dented, smooth, rough, pinch, press.

Discussion

Sharing for responses can take place when the pieces are not permanent or intended for firing. After a shape or object has been modelled, the teacher or peers may ask questions such as:

Tell me about your shape/object?

Does your shape/object have a name?

I don't understand what this part is; can you tell me more about it?

Would you like to change any part?

Would you like to add anything to the shape/object?

Discussion may arise during or after making the piece and the techniques used to produce various effects can be discussed.

How did you make this shape?

What did you use to make this mark?

What do these marks remind you of?

How does this feel?

How did you make it?

Could you make it again?

Discuss possible methods of changing a piece as children develop their own techniques; for example, cutting a piece off, adding a piece by joining, pinching or squeezing part or all of the piece, scratching with a tool.

Crafting and Presenting

The children could use clay:
- to make wind chimes using pinch pots and balls of clay. Bisque fire. To decorate, spray with gold, silver or fluorescent colour OR polish with a cloth and coloured shoe polish OR paint with acrylic colour and gloss with clear varnish
- to make a tile using a slab of clay. Decorate with texture tools, then bisque fire. Finish off with one of the methods used for the wind chimes.

(Any object that can be hollowed out to allow drying may be chosen for firing.)

CLAY-MODELLING
Phase 2

LEARNING OBJECTIVES

1 Children will produce a piece that can be viewed and discussed by others.
2 Children will make use of the techniques of hand-building including the additive, substractive, pinch and slab methods.
3 Children will extend their techniques of hand-building to include bas-relief and egg-base.
4 Children will be aware of the coil method of hand-building.
5 Children will become familiar with a variety of joining techniques.
6 Children will learn how to care for the clay and modelling equipment.
7 Children will employ texturing techniques to enhance meaning, using a variety of materials and modelling tools.
8 Children will become familiar with language relating to clay: model, modelling, tool, solid, form, join, texture, pattern, coil, hollow, slab, stamp, surface, addition, subtraction, pound, egg-base, cylinder, cone.

LEARNING EXPERIENCES

Getting Started

Shape clay
Use balls of clay and discover ways of changing the shape of the clay—by rolling, pulling, twisting, pinching, joining, pounding, cutting, hollowing, scratching, flattening.

Explore techniques
Discover which technique works best to make shapes that are: round, long, lumpy, flat, square, curled and so on.

Discuss the children's discoveries and record them.

    I made a flat shape by pounding.

    I made a round shape by rolling.

    I made the clay lumpy by pinching and pulling.

Experiment with tools
Use simple hand-building tools such as a knife, sticks and nails. Experiment with these to discover how they can be used: to draw on clay, to make marks in clay, to make the clay feel different, to smooth the clay out.

Look at clay products
Look at the various uses of clay such as in bricks and pottery. Make a display of pottery (functional and decorative) for the children to feel, observe and discuss.

Blind modelling
Cover a ball of clay with paper or put it in a paper bag and model it 'blind'. Remove the paper to reveal the surprise shape.

    Blindfold children and ask them to make the clay lumpy, dented, smooth, rough, textured.

Join clay
Experiment with the various methods of joining clay—by smoothly scraping surfaces, by adding a little water, by pressing pieces together and smoothing over the joins with the fingers.

Developing Concepts and Techniques

Experiences and techniques from Phase 1 are reviewed and developed. Additional methods are introduced gradually.

Review and development activities

Revise the additive, subtractive, pinch and slab methods of construction (see page 29).

Extend the pinch method to make an egg-base.

Egg-base method
Make two pinched pots of even size.
Join them to create a hollow egg-shape.

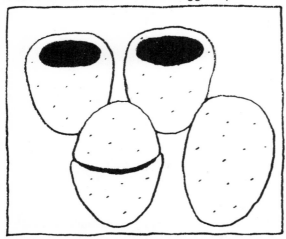

Extend the slab method to make a bas-relief.

Bas-relief method
Start with a slab of clay. Then add or subtract shapes and pieces of clay.

Introduce the coil method.

Coil method
Roll out coils of clay using the palms of the hands. (Stress that the coils should be even.) Use the coils for building.

Use texture
Texture can be created with: a variety of found objects (stones, seeds, bark, twigs, leaves), a variety of man-made objects (nails, wire, buttons, modelling tools).

Press clay into surfaces such as bark, rocks and brick walls to reveal texture.

Joining activities
Show the children a variety of joining techniques to use in their pieces; for example, the socket join where you build a new form by making holes in a piece of clay and placing shapes into these holes. Use matches or pieces of wire to join clay.

The various texture and joining techniques can be used by children to enhance their pieces.

Discussion
As in Phase 1, encourage the children to discuss their efforts with each other. As always, questions should focus initially on the content, and then on the techniques.

What is your piece about?
Tell me about this part.
Does your piece have a name?
How did you make the piece?
What method did you use?
Could you add to the piece in any way?
Would you like to change something?

Discussion of the techniques and effects may proceed as follows.

How did you join this piece to that?
What did you use to make these marks?
How does this improve your piece?
Do you think this join will last?
How does the object feel and look now that you have added texture?
Why did you add this piece/these marks?

Crafting and Presenting

The children could use clay:
- to make tiles or jewellery using the bas-relief method
- to make bells by using a pinched pot joined to a coil of clay. Decorate with texture tools (natural and man-made). Bisque fire and finish off using shoe polish, wood stains, diluted oil paints, acrylic paint or water paint and varnish.

CLAY-MODELLING
Phase 3

LEARNING OBJECTIVES

1 Children will display an understanding of the techniques of hand-building—the additive, subtractive, pinch, slab, coil and bas-relief methods.
2 Children will employ a variety of joining techniques, including the use of 'slip' (a creamy mixture of clay and water), in their pieces.
3 Children will refine their methods of hand-building with the use of 'slip'.
4 Children will gain confidence in their employment of techniques and show a willingness to discuss appropriate uses of these.
5 Children will use a variety of modelling tools and materials, including 'slip', to enhance the meaning of their pieces.
6 Children will work a piece, refine it and present it to an audience.
7 Children will become familiar with language relating to clay: decorate, slip, support, strength, balance, stable, relief, two-dimensional, three-dimensional, firing, bisque, pottery, potter, sculptor, ceramics.

LEARNING EXPERIENCES

Getting Started

Discuss pottery
Use a display of pottery to discuss various aspects of the craft with the children such as: functional and decorative pottery, hand-built pottery and pottery made on a wheel.

Ask questions such as:

What or who is a potter?
Where do potters work?
Are we potters?
Is a sculptor a potter?
What are ceramics?
Can we use pottery?
Do we use all pieces?
How can pottery be made?

Talk to potters
Visit a pottery, or invite a potter to talk to the children about the craft.

Make clay shapes
Use balls of clay and techniques such as rolling, pulling, pinching, pounding, cutting, hollowing, and allow the children to discover ways of making a variety of shaped pieces: balls, flattened pancakes, long coils, twisted pieces, curled pieces, irregular pieces, abstract pieces, realistic pieces and so on.

Shapes in sequence
Practise manipulating the clay by introducing a variety of shapes in sequence; for example, roll a ball—make a block—make a cylinder—change it to a cone—make it a pyramid—now a snake.

Join clay
Practise joining clay using the fingers and clay tools to smooth over the joins.

Use 'slip'
Show the children how to moisten some clay to make 'slip' which can be used as a joining agent.

Record the children's responses. 'Slip' is: creamy, wet, slimy, smooth.

Practise joining the clay using 'slip'—by joining two 'sausage' shapes together, joining a ball of clay to a 'sausage' shape.

Developing Concepts and Techniques

It is important that children get their ideas down quickly without concentrating too heavily on correct methods and techniques. When children concentrate heavily on correct techniques and labour over a piece in the early stages, they are often reluctant to change or expand it as it develops.

At this stage the teacher should show children how to develop ideas by
- listening, probing and suggesting
- admiring, encouraging and praising
- creating with the children
- watching for those who need help
- building on what they can already do.

During this Phase the techniques and methods are practised and developed to enable the children to express their ideas and feelings freely.

Review and development activities

Use the following hand-building methods: additive and subtractive, pinch, slab, coil, bas-relief.

Joining activities

Extend the use of the various joining techniques such as: joining by pushing and moulding pieces together, joining using matches or wire, joining using 'slip'.

Join two pinched pots to make an egg-base.

Join a slab to a coil by making a round slab and applying 'slip' to the edge. The coil can then be placed around the edge. Build the coils up, applying 'slip' to each layer.

Modelling activities and texture

Extend the use of texture tools to add meaning to a piece; for example, you could add scales, hair, warts, facial features, patterns, decoration.

Produce texture by using a variety of natural and man-made tools including hessian, nails, flywire, corrugated card, twigs, stones.

Discussion

During the crafting process encourage the children to look at their own pieces and to develop a self-evaluation formula.

Sharing with peers provides new insights and helps to clarify ideas.

Do you like my piece?
Do you think I could change anything?

Is there anything you don't understand?
Is there any detail you think I should add?

Discuss the ideas, how the piece developed, the techniques and methods used. As a result of sharing for responses, children naturally change and extend pieces. They may expand pieces and add more detail, subtract or add bits, use a different method or technique, reject the piece and begin again.

Teacher's strategies include: displaying a piece to work on collectively, spotlighting the children's efforts at revision, comparing the children's techniques with the craftsperson's model.

Crafting and Presenting

The children could use clay:
- to make egg-base creatures or animals by adding appendages and features such as horns, googly eyes, clawed feet, ears and so on. Texture to show scales, hair, warts, nails, feathers. Prepare the piece by inserting air holes to allow drying. Bisque fire and decorate using one of the methods described in Phases 1 or 2

- to make small coil pots, with either straight or sloping sides. The coils may be smoothed over or textured or left as they are

- to make a box, dish, tile or plaque using slabs.

CLAY-MODELLING
Phase 4

LEARNING OBJECTIVES

1 Children will make wide use of the various techniques of hand-building: additive and subtractive, pinch, slab, coil, bas-relief, egg-base and drape-mould methods.
2 Children will select the most useful technique(s) to create a piece.
3 Children will learn the technique of kneading or wedging the clay prior to use.
4 Children will plan and develop a piece(s) and present it to an audience.
5 Children will refine their techniques in decorating pieces prior to and after firing.
6 Children will become familiar with language relating to clay: wedge, knead, drape, leather hard, cultural style(s), personal style(s), durable, functional, decoration, aesthetic, kiln, kiln stilts, kiln shelves, oven ware, fire brick, earthenware, stoneware, porcelain.

LEARNING EXPERIENCES

Getting Started

Discuss pottery

Study the ceramic ware of ancient times and consider the shapes, decorations, methods of construction and uses of the pieces.

Look at clay as a medium for making jewellery. Study prints, pictures or films of tribal people who make pottery jewellery.

Compare the pottery of today with ancient pottery. Invite the children to bring along functional and decorative pieces to display and discuss with each other. Points for discussion may be:

Is this piece useful or decorative?

Does it serve its purpose well?

How could it have been made?

Would the craftsperson be a potter or a sculptor?

What is meant by cultural style(s) and personal style(s)?

Evaluative questions may include:

If bricks are made of clay which has been fired, why do we value pottery more highly than bricks?

Is functional or decorative pottery more highly valued?

See potters in action

Visit a pottery, or invite a potter or sculptor to talk to the children.

Manipulate clay

Practise the various methods of manipulating the clay by making: coils, balls, flat pieces, irregular shapes, realistic shapes, pieces with textured surfaces, pinched pieces and so on.

Ask the children to compose a sequence such as: ball — pinched pot — cone — coil — rolled coil — flattened pancake (slab).

Join clay

Practise joining clay using 'slip'.

Developing Concepts and Techniques

Children in this Phase are being guided towards independence. They should be developing the ability to make judgements and decisions about content, concepts and techniques and the likely communicative effectiveness of their pieces. They should also be developing their personal styles and methods to suit their purposes.

Review and development activities

Use the methods of hand-building previously discussed: additive and subtractive, pinch, slab, coil, bas-relief, egg-base.

Extend the use of slabs to include the drape-mould method of construction.

Drape-mould

Prepare a thin slab of clay.
Cover the mould with newspaper, cloth or plastic wrap to prevent sticking and to ease removal of the clay.

Press the clay gently over the mould.

Remove the clay when it is leather hard.

Suitable moulds are: bottles (with straight sides to allow the bottle to be removed), bowls (coils can be laid in the bowl in various patterns), jars (under 15 cm high with straight sides).

Joining activities

Use the various joining techniques, including the use of 'slip'.

Extend the use of 'slip'; use it as a method of decoration and to create texture. For example, you could apply different coloured 'slips' or apply 'slip' and then scratch through it.

Discussion

Once children are familiar with these methods and techniques they can experiment with partial pieces, discuss how the piece will develop and, from their experience with the 'tries', decide on the most suitable direction to take.

The teacher's role is to offer encouragement and support and to guide the children gently towards a process of self-examination.

What will my piece be (about)?
How will I begin?
What methods and techniques should I use?
Which part is showing the most promise?
How can I build on this?
What's good in this piece?

Guide the children to evaluate their own work through purposeful questioning.

What did the other children think of your piece?
Could you have created the piece using a different method?
Can your piece be used?
Did you create the best effect you could?
Who did you create the piece for?
Is there something here that you could use again?
How does this piece compare with other pieces?
Would you like to preserve this piece?

Crafting and Presenting

The children could create a piece using any method they prefer, making their own decisions about how it should be decorated prior to bisque firing. Following is a sample preparation sheet.

Name_____ Grade_____

- Make your choice *before* you come to the next session.
- Make your choice *carefully*—you know your own ability.
- You are responsible for your own equipment—mould, texture tools (natural or man-made).
- Place a tick beside the piece you wish to make.

PINCH POTS
1 Monsters, creatures
2 Money box
3 Wind chimes
Requirements: texture tools

COILS
1 Coil pot with straight sides, textured
2 As for 1 with a lid
3 Shaped coil pot, textured
4 As for 3, but smoothed with a knife
5 Either 1 or 3, using a mould
6 Coil in a bowl mould
Requirements: texture tools, mould, newspaper, old tea towel

SLABS
1 Flower pot
2 Vase, using a mould
3 Bottle
4 Jewellery
5 Tiles
6 Plate
Requirements: texture tools, mould, newspaper, old tea towel

While the pieces are set to dry, give the children instruction on:
- how the kiln works
- loading and unloading the kiln.

Their pieces can be decorated using one of the methods outlined in the previous Phases or by glazing.

Glazes
A glaze is a liquid coating whose special glass component seals the surface of the clay so that it becomes non-porous (waterproof).

Be sure that no glaze is on the bottom of the object as it will stick to the kiln during firing. Sponge off any excess glaze with water.

Below are the various methods of applying glaze.

Dipping
Stir the glaze thoroughly so that it has an even consistency, then dip the object into the glaze at an angle. The glaze should not be too thick. Touch up uncoloured spots with a paint brush. Drip designs look very interesting (dip and drip).

Pouring
Pour the glaze over and around the object. Pour quickly to stop the glaze thickening. To glaze the inside of a pot, pour in the glaze and rotate the pot quickly.

Brushing
With a *wide, soft* brush apply coats of glaze in various directions. To produce even bands of colour, you could rotate the pot on a turntable. To produce patterns, you could brush the pot with hot wax and then dip it in the glaze (wax resist) or apply glaze through a stencil.

Spraying
Instead of using a brush you could spray glazes on.

TEXTILES
Phase 1

LEARNING OBJECTIVES

1 Children will be introduced to and explore a variety of fabrics and threads through matching and sorting.
2 Children will learn the methods of joining threads and fabrics by tying and gluing.
3 Children will construct and decorate threads and fabrics.
4 Children will use fabrics and threads in picture-making.
5 Children will share their experiences and discuss their efforts with others.
6 Children will become familiar with language relating to textiles: fabric, thread, cloth, clothes, material, rough, smooth, see-through, patterned, furry, prickly, spongy, thick, thin, wool, cotton, string, nylon, yarn, cord, rope, tape, raffia, twine, hayband, length, tie, knot, pin, fray, fringe, cut, clothing (skirt, dress, coat etc.) costume, uniform.

LEARNING EXPERIENCES

Getting Started

Introduce cloth

Introduce and explore a variety of types of fabrics. You could use cloth scraps and old clothes. Factories and craft and haberdashery suppliers are good sources.

The collections should include materials of different weights, colours, patterns, textures and methods of manufacture.

The children can discover and select fabrics: bright happy colours; soft, smooth cloth; thick, rough material; sheer materials; brightly patterned cloth and so on.

Record their responses. Make charts like the ones below.

CLOTH CAN BE -
- rough   · smooth
- thick   · prickly
- bumpy   · patterned
- thin   · colourful
- spongy · woolly
- furry   · textured

Introduce thread

Introduce and explore a variety of types of threads. Once again the collections should include threads of different lengths, thicknesses and methods of manufacture.

Compile lists of the children's responses. Make charts like the one below.

TYPES OF THREAD -
- wool   · cotton
- cord   · string
- rope   · raffia
- tape   · hayband
- nylon · twine

Group fabrics and threads

Ask the children to group the fabrics and threads according to preference.

> Which piece do you like the best?
> Why?

Pin the fabric and thread 'collections' to a display board. The theme of the collection can be changed: green fabrics, warm fabrics, fabrics I like to feel, threads that are made up of other threads.

Look at how fabrics are made

Explore simple open-weave fabrics and threads. The children can pull threads to discover the weave.

Textiles in the environment

Examine fabrics and threads found in the children's environment: curtains in the classroom, wool in a child's jumper, stitching on a dress, carpet and so on.

Dress up

Provide a 'dressing up' corner and box containing different clothes such as gowns, overalls and uniforms. Also include large pieces of fabric and threads so that the children can practise joining methods using safety pins, threads (for tying) and elastic (for securing hats, masks).

Practise simple activities with threads such as the tying of knots (with shoe laces and hair ribbons, on parcels).

Provide a context for the children through questions.

> Who are you dressing up as?
> What is he/she wearing? Why?
> Can you write a story about what he/she is doing?

Discuss clothes

Visit a shopping complex to observe the various ways in which people dress; for example, the butcher, women shoppers, shop assistants and so on.

Discuss fabrics and clothes generally.

> Why do we wear clothes?
> What types of clothes do you have?
> How do we use fabrics in our homes?
> How do we use animals to make our clothes?

Developing Concepts and Techniques

Through class and group discussions lead the children to understand how threads and fabrics can be used to create designs and pictures.

Questioning may proceed as follows.

> How can you use fabric to make a picture?
> How can you use threads to 'draw' a picture?
> How can threads and fabrics be arranged on a piece of paper or cardboard?
> Can you arrange threads and fabrics to make a picture to touch?
> How can you change (or decorate) a piece of fabric?
> How can you change (or decorate) a thread?

Activities with threads

Make knots: a small knot, a large knot, a knot with a loop, knots that are close together or far apart, lots of knots on top of each other, knots to join two or more cords together.

Combine threads to make new threads by twisting together or by knotting.

Decorate a thread by fraying, knotting, adding beads, seeds or gum nuts.

Thread thick threads into coarse-meshed fabrics using fingers, paper clips or bobby pins to thread with.

Activities with fabrics

Cut or tear various types of fabrics.
Cut fabric into shapes.
Cut shapes into pieces of fabric.
Fringe or fray the edge of the fabric shape.
Pull some threads from the fabric to make lines.
Draw on fabric with permanent felt-tip pens.
Glue fabric to paper or cardboard.

Activities with fabrics and threads

Twist and curl the threads to make the outline of an object (for example, an animal) or shape.
Cut a shape from the fabric and add some thread to decorate it.
Cut one shape from the fabric and place a different shape over the top with a thread.
Cut shapes of fabric and strips of thread then arrange them to make a pattern.
Cut shapes of fabric and then decorate them with thread.
Glue fabrics and threads to paper or cardboard.

Discussion

Encourage the children to discuss their 'pictures' with others at various stages during the process. It is often important for the children to discuss their ideas before the pieces of fabric or thread are permanently joined or fixed together. With most activities the children can simply experiment without producing a permanent or final product.
Discuss both the composing process and any finished pieces. Sharing time may proceed as follows.

What shapes of fabric or pieces of thread have you cut?
How can the pieces be arranged on the paper?
Which colours look best together?
Tell us about your picture.
Does it tell a story?

Questions may be asked to clarify content.

What is this part?
Tell us more about this part?
What part do you like best?

Techniques can then be highlighted.

How did you make this piece?
How did you fix these pieces together?
How did you overlap these shapes?

Crafting and Presenting

The children could use fabrics and threads:
• to make a 'touch' picture using fabric
• to make a 'touch' picture using fabrics and threads
• to make a piece by threading thick thread through open-weave fabric; for example, onion sacking
• to enhance a model (masks, puppets) or decorate a book cover or card
• to illustrate techniques of knotting, fraying, fringing, cutting and so on
• to illustrate an idea or story before or after writing.

TEXTILES
Phase 2

LEARNING OBJECTIVES

1 Children will match and sort fabrics and threads according to colour, texture, length/size, shape.
2 Children will examine how fabrics and threads are constructed.
3 Children will be introduced to the idea of weaving.
4 Children will learn the joining methods of gluing, tying, pinning and sewing.
5 Children will change and modify threads and fabrics by knotting, fringing, fraying and pulling threads.
6 Children will learn simple methods of stitching (running stitch, cross stitch).
7 Children will become familiar with language relating to textiles: match, sort, sew, bond, staple, stitch, unravel, hessian, onion sacking, pom pom, tassel, loop, twist, under, over, woven, running stitch, cross stitch, plaiting, draw (meaning pull), fold, gather, beads, buttons, sequins.

LEARNING EXPERIENCES

Getting Started

Explore fabrics and threads

Examine collections of fabrics and threads. Through various tactile and visual experiences, the children can sort and classify the materials according to colour, pattern, shape, texture and so on. Discuss aspects such as:

How do fabrics/threads look and feel?

What are their similarities and differences?

How do textures contrast with one another (rough — smooth, shiny — dull)?

How are patterns similar to one another?

How do patterns differ (regular — irregular, bright — dull, large — small)?

Discuss different materials

Encourage the children to bring along samples of fabrics and threads. Then try to categorize them according to the material type (cotton, woollen, synthetic).

Discuss the origins and uses of fibres. For example, you could observe silkworms spinning a cocoon.

Pull materials apart

Unravel pieces of fabric and thread to see how they are made. Materials such as onion sacking, hessian, knitted and crocheted pieces, rope and cord may be pulled apart and examined.

Introduce weaving

Weave with paper strips to demonstrate the idea of making fabrics.

Thread materials through chicken wire, onion sacking, a peg board or a wire fence stressing the over/under technique or movement.

Join fabrics

Explore and discuss the different methods of joining fabrics and threads such as pinning, sewing, stapling, darning, bonding, gluing, tying.

Look at pieces of clothing to examine the ways pieces of fabric are joined, or objects (buttons, studs) are joined to fabric. Look at the stitches used, the types of threads and so on.

Explore the different properties of fabrics

Examine the effects of colour applied to fabrics by painting with food dye or thin paint.

Test for colour fastness by using a bleach.

Look at the washability of clothing. Why is some clothing marked 'handwash' or 'dry clean only'.

Examine the effects of burning and refer to the safety warning on nightware.

Developing Concepts and Techniques

Previously learned techniques can be applied in problem-solving situations and further techniques can be introduced as the need arises.

Thread activities

Provide the children with quick problem-solving exercises.

Change a thread by knotting.

Change a thread by cutting and fraying.

Add to a thread by combining it with other threads by twisting or plaiting.

Add to a thread by decorating it with beads, buttons, sequins and other collected items.

Knot pieces of thread together to make a pattern.

Dip pieces of thread in glue and apply them to paper or cardboard or to three-dimensional forms such as bottles, clay pieces and polystyrene.

Show the children the methods of making pom poms and tassels.

Pom pom

Cut two cardboard circles of equal size.

Cut identical holes in the circles and place them together.

Wrap some thread through the centre hole and around both pieces of cardboard many times.

Cut the thread along the outside edge.

Tie a long piece of thread between the two pieces of cardboard.

Remove the cardboard and tie securely.

Tassel

Cut a small square of cardboard and run a piece of thread or cord along the top edge.

Wrap some thread around the centre of the cardboard about twelve times.

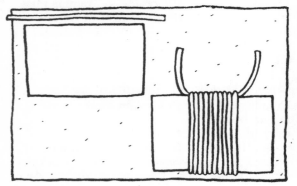

Cut the threads along the bottom edge of the cardboard.

Tie a cord tightly a short space from the top to form the tassel.

Draw threads

Create texture by pulling threads. To do this, pull the threads horizontally or vertically (pull several, about ten, next to each other). This will leave open window spaces; these can be pinched and tied off in clusters, glued open, or simply left as designs.

Remove threads from the edge (fringing).

Remove threads to make lines across the fabric.

Remove threads to make thick and thin lines.

Remove threads to make a cross.

Mix different fabrics

Experiment with the placement of cloth considering colours, patterns, textures and shapes. Proceed through questions such as:

Which colours look the best close together?

Do patterned fabrics need to be next to plain fabrics?

How can the shapes be arranged in the piece?

How can the texture of the fabrics be varied?

Make a fabric picture

Give the children time to sketch ideas on paper first, and to sketch the design patterns on fabric, before cutting out the final designs.

The pieces need to be removed, replaced and changed before moving to a final product using the following method.

Fabric picture

Glue down a slightly larger backing cloth on to cardboard. Allow the cloth to extend over the edges of the cardboard. Fold the fabric under and glue.

Cut, glue and press down each piece on to the backing.

Add yarns and beads for decoration. Draw on details with permanent felt-tip pens.

Cover the entire cloth with waxed paper. Press the picture with a heavy object such as a book until it is dry.

Fabric and thread activities

Introduce some simple stitching methods.

Running stitch

This is a common stitch used for hemming or tacking a piece of cloth.

To make a stitch pass the needle through the cloth under and out a short distance along. You can take several stitches on the needle at once and pull the needle through the cloth. Stitches can be made along a straight or a curved line and should be even.

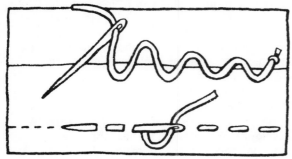

Cross stitch

Make a series of diagonal stitches by passing the needle through, under and out of the cloth. Work back across these stitches with the opposite diagonal stitch to make crosses.

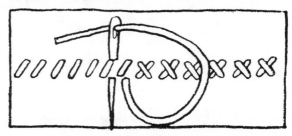

Spend time experimenting with different stitches and encourage the children to invent their own stitches. They can practise on plastic mesh or hessian using thick thread and a blanket needle. When there are no preconceived plans or established goals, the children will enjoy the experience more.

Encourage the children to add to or to change their pieces through discussion questions.

How did you make that stitch?

Can you make another to join to it?

Can you make a pattern of stitches?

Can you join fabrics by stitching?

Can you add an object such as a button or a bead by stitching?

Can you make a stitch on top of another stitch?

Crafting and Presenting

The children could use fabrics and threads:
- to make a picture
- to make a patchwork picture. Cut scraps of cloth into geometric shapes. Be sure to cut them so they fit together like a puzzle
- to make a 'touch' picture in which various materials such as cloth, string and wool are stuck on to a surface
- to make a mural. Leave a large piece of hessian or linen out for children to add stitches, pieces of found materials, collected objects and so on. The giant mural is also a record of the children's discoveries. Others can use the ideas expressed in the mural for their own pieces
- to illustrate techniques; for example, by making pom-pom toys and wool dollies
- to decorate models (masks, puppets), book covers and cards.

TEXTILES
Phase 3

LEARNING OBJECTIVES

1 Children will consolidate and extend their techniques of stitching, knotting and weaving.
2 Children will learn more about the methods of stitching (backstitch, couching stitch, satin stitch, blanket stitch).
3 Children will learn simple knotting techniques.
4 Children will begin simple loom weaving.
5 Children will use a variety of materials and techniques to create three-dimensional pieces.
6 Children will discuss the design qualities of their pieces (texture, colour, pattern, shape, space).
7 Children will become familiar with language relating to textiles: curtains, furnishings, dye, knitted, crocheted, fibres (animal, vegetable, mineral), hand-made, machine-made, weaving, woven, loom, warp (skeleton or framework of fabric), weft (the threads that cross over and under and are woven into the warp threads), shuttle (device that carries yarn over and under the warp), beater (used to push the woven thread into place), backstitch, couching stitch, satin stitch, square knot, half-hitch, mounting knot, stuff, pleat, gather.

LEARNING EXPERIENCES

Getting Started

Examine fabrics

Examine some fabrics and threads using a magnifying glass or a microscope to discover the methods of construction.

Pull apart loosely woven hessian or onion sacking to discover what the fabric is made of and how.

Examine nets, string bags and lace to see how they are made.

Unravel knitted or crocheted fabric and material such as cord, rope, twine or string.

Visit places where fabrics are displayed

Visit display homes or furniture shops to look at the furnishing fabrics. Discuss their tastefulness and durability.

Visit department stores to look at clothing and fabric.

Discuss the types of fibres

Animal fibres: wool, hair, silk, leather
Vegetable fibres: cotton, flax, jute
Mineral fibres: glass, metallic yarns

What are some of the different names we call fabrics? threads?

Why are fabrics made in different ways?

Are hand-made fabrics superior to machine-made fabrics?

Study clothes

Discuss clothes for different purposes: special occasions, uniforms, sports clothes, overalls, party dress-ups.

Study national costumes and clothes through the ages.

Demonstrate the weaving process

Have ten children stand in a line with the first child holding one end of a rope. Place the rope in front of the first student behind the next, in front of the next and so on. Go back alternating front and back to illustrate the weaving process.

Discuss the tradition of weaving

Look at weaving as one of the first crafts developed by people. The basis of weaving — the rhythmic movements over and under, and in and out—and the basic design of the loom have not changed much throughout history.

Look at woven pieces such as baskets, tapestries and mats. Point out that other creatures such as birds and insects also weave.

Make collections

Collect materials such as old jewellery, buttons, wooden and glass beads, braid, sequins, bells and found objects which can be used later in fabric and thread work.

Developing Concepts and Techniques

The children could create or compose pieces quickly so that they can experiment with and practise previously learned techniques of working with threads and fabrics. It is important that value is placed on all these efforts and that the final product is not always the priority.

At this stage techniques of stitching, knotting and weaving are consolidated and extended through the following activities.

Stitching activities

Revise previously learned stitches (running stitch, cross stitch; see page 43). Through problem-solving activities, introduce the children to further simple methods.

Make a line of stitches with spaces.
Make a line of stitches without spaces.
Make stitches with loops.
Make crosses with stitches.
Use stitches to fill in a space.

Backstitch

Make one running stitch.

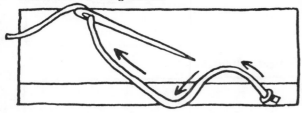

On the next stitch go back to fill in the space.

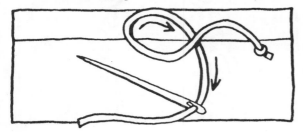

Underneath move twice the distance along and back through the cloth.

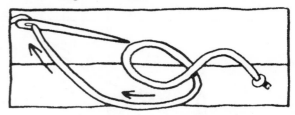

Once again go back and fill in the space.

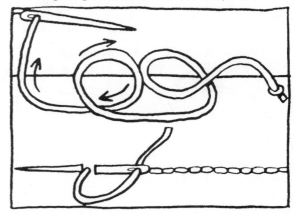

Couching stitch

Lay the yarn to be embroidered on the cloth. With a needle and thread stitch the yarn by bringing the needle up on one side, across, and down through to the back on the other side. This holds the yarn firmly in place.

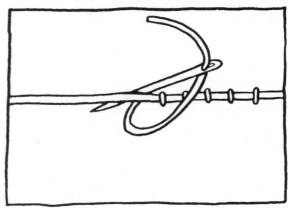

Satin stitch

Satin stitch is used to fill in designs.
Use small running stitches spaced next to each other to fill in an already designed shape.
This filling in also puts the stitches in relief, giving the finished work bulk.
Space the stitches close to each other, as shown.

Blanket stitch

Bring the needle and thread from underneath to the front of the cloth.

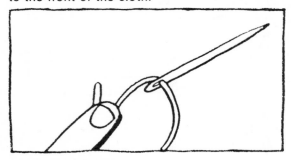

Make half a loop with the thread and hold it with the thumb.

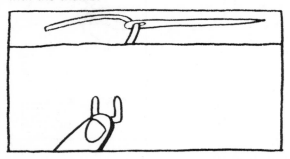

Go through to the underside of the cloth and still hold the thread to make a right angle

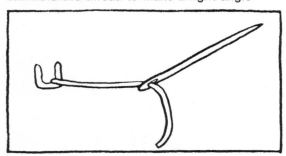

Come up through the cloth at the point of the angle and repeat the process.

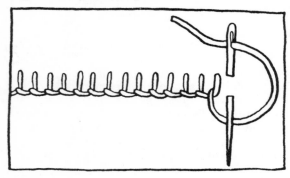

Knotting activities

Build on the informal knot-tying experiences of the previous Phases by introducing the children to some formal knotting methods.

Setting on or mounting the cords

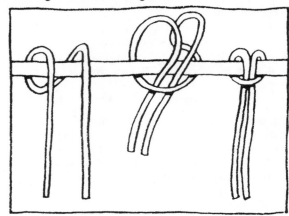

Horizontal cording

double half-hitch to left

double half-hitch to right

Vertical half-hitches

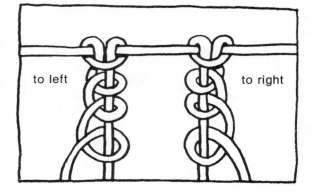

to left   to right

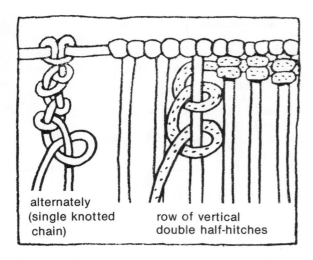

alternately
(single knotted
chain)

row of vertical
double half-hitches

The square knot

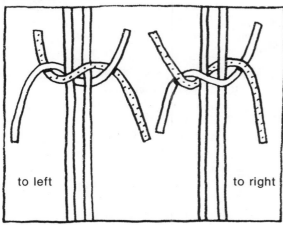

to left

to right

The double half-hitch knot

Repeat a number of square knots for chain.
For twist just repeat half (a) of square knot.

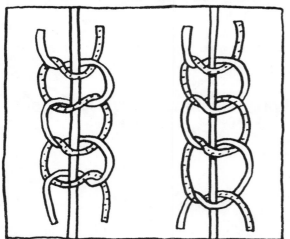

Once the children have learned these knots
they can try to discover ways of combining
them or using them in a way no one else has.

Weaving activities
Now that the children have had weaving
experiences with prepared 'boards' (chicken
wire, onion sacking, wire fences), they can
begin simple loom weaving.

Cardboard loom
Cut slits into the top and bottom edges of a
piece of cardboard.
Place the warp threads through the slits.
Then weave or thread other threads through
the warp.
When completed the fabric may be removed
from the loom and used.

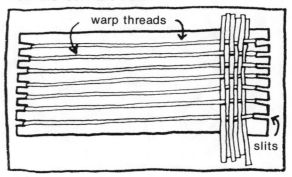

warp threads

slits

Box loom
This is based on the same principle as the
cardboard loom above, but the warp threads
are attached to slits in an open-topped box.

Drinking-straw loom
Weave weft threads over and under drinking
straws.
When the length of the straw is completed,
slide the straws further down the warp threads
and continue.

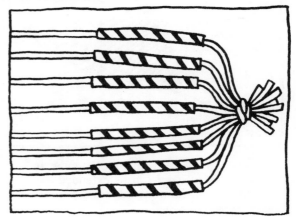

Picture-frame loom

Put nails into opposite ends of an old picture frame.

The warp threads are wound around the nails.

The weft threads are threaded on to the warp.

Take the nails out when the weaving is completed.

Bike-wheel loom

Use the spokes of a wheel as the warp threads.

Thread other threads through these to make circular designs.

Children can decorate their own bicycles.

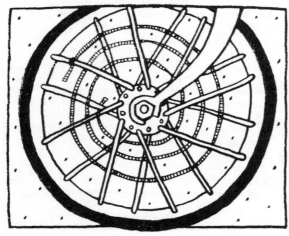

Branch loom

The warp threads are wound around a forked branch.

The weft threads are woven into these.

This is good group project when a large branch, with many forks, is used.

Weaving activities with simple looms and various types of wool can be extended to incorporate natural materials such as grass, leaves, sticks and shells.

Make three-dimensional forms

The techniques of working with textiles (stitching, knotting, weaving and so on) can be used to create simple three-dimensional forms. Fabric pieces can be pleated, rolled, padded, gathered and folded. These can then be joined to make objects in the shape of people and animals. Buttons, beads and threads can be used to add features and/or details to the pieces.

Stockings, socks or tubes of fabric can be stuffed (with crumpled newspaper, cotton wool or stockings) and modelled into shapes. Details and features can be added with buttons, beads, threads and so on.

Discussion

Discussion of the children's pieces should focus on the ideas, how the piece developed and the techniques used.

Here are some sample questions.

Tell us about your piece.

Does the piece have a name or title?

What was your initial idea?

How long have you been working on the piece?

How did the piece develop?

What materials did you use other than threads and fabrics?

What stitching or knotting techniques did you use?

How did you add detail to the piece?

Did you discover something you could use again?

Crafting and Presenting

The children could use fabrics and threads:
• to make three-dimensional forms such as dolls, toys, puppets

Sock puppets

Fold the toe section in to form a 'mouth'. Add a tongue, eyes, hair and so on to create characters.

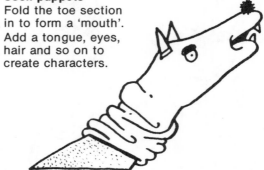

48

Glove puppets

Stocking-face doll

Stuff a nylon stocking with other stockings.
With a needle and thread start sewing facial
features.
Catch some of the stuffing with the outside
fabric as you stitch, pulling the stitches
together to create a three-dimensional
sculptured face. Children are surprised and
delighted as the funny features develop.

Stuffed toys

Stuff a square of
fabric.
Tie it with a rubber
band or thread.
Pieces of cloth,
threads, beads,
buttons and so on
can be used to add
detail and special
features.

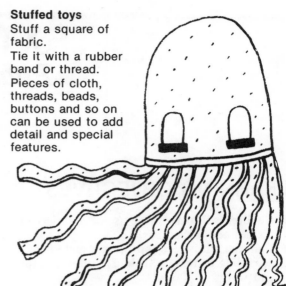

- to make macramé plant hangers, belts, dog
  leads, jewellery and wall hangings
- to make a cushion using a large piece of
  weaving sewn to a square/rectangle of
  hessian and stuffed
- to create and decorate special areas in the
  classroom. Use threads and fabrics to
  decorate spaces or create a thread jungle or
  web. Combine and attach the fabrics and
  threads so they remain in place and fill the
  area. They may be supported by: cardboard
  boxes, chairs or stools, branches of trees,
  fences (a fenced outdoor courtyard is ideal),
  bicycle wheels. Children can use a variety of
  techniques to complete this activity.

TEXTILES
Phase 4

LEARNING OBJECTIVES

1 Children will make wide use of a variety of textiles and techniques.
2 Children will select appropriate materials according to texture, colour, pattern, shape and so on.
3 Children will review and refine methods of weaving, knotting and stitching.
4 Children will plan, develop and present a piece using various materials and techniques.
5 Children will make fabrics by knitting and crocheting.
6 Children will decorate fabrics using tie-dye, batik and appliqué techniques.
7 Children will become familiar with language relating to textiles: spinning, weaving, macramé, tapestry, mat, braid, basketry, patchwork, appliqué, embroidery, needlecraft, knit (cast on, cast off, plain, purl, rib, ply), crochet (hook, double, chain, treble), wax, resist, dye, absorb, penetrate, wall hanging, flag, banner, tie-dye, batik.

LEARNING EXPERIENCES

Getting Started

Examine textiles in history
Make a display of pictures showing examples of the ancient needle-and-thread crafts such as embroidery, patchwork, appliqué and tapestry. Discuss the methods, materials and tools used in these crafts.

Discuss how people have always used these techniques to adorn clothes and household objects such as quilts. Adornment has played a major part in almost every culture and studying examples is an excellent way to learn about the history and the art of a people.

Discuss decorative textiles
Examine and discuss fabric pieces such as flags, banners and hangings used as festive additions on special occasions. We find them displayed in galleries, homes and churches. Discussion should centre on the composition and design qualities of such pieces and the ideas behind them.

Arrange demonstrations
Invite crafts people to talk to the children and to demonstrate and display crafts such as spinning and weaving, macramé, basketry and rug making.

Invite elderly citizens or visit some elderly citizens to observe and discuss crafts with threads and fabrics such as knitting, tapestry, crochet, embroidery and appliqué.

Discuss dyeing techniques
Make a display of pieces decorated using tie-dye or batik methods. The collection may include pieces of fabric, clothing (such as a scarf, shirt or blouse), wall hangings and murals.

Study the traditional Indonesian craft of batik: the materials and tools they use and the traditional designs created.

Developing Concepts and Techniques
Children in this Phase should be encouraged to use the wide variety of textiles and techniques outlined in the earlier Phases. They also need to make choices concerning the content, materials, tools and techniques used in their pieces. They will have to make decisions about aspects such as variations in fabric textures, colour relationships, the use of plain or patterned fabrics, contrasting lights and darks, and so on. Through experimenting, selecting and planning, pieces can be crafted and presented to an audience.

Designs can also be planned on paper indicating colours, textures and shapes. The artists may ask themselves:

What qualities am I trying to achieve?

What materials match these desired qualities?

What is the durability and availability (cost) of these materials?

What techniques of stitching, knotting or weaving will I use?

What materials do I need besides threads and fabrics?

To extend the children beyond the simple methods of stitching, weaving and knotting outlined in the previous Phases, more elaborate methods of decoration and fabric-making are introduced.

Fabric decoration activities

Use the tie-dye method.

Tie-dyeing

Fabric can by dyed in one (or a combination) of the following ways:
- by knotting the fabric tightly
- by pegging or clipping the fabric in various places
- by bunching the fabric together and tying it in various places with string, cotton or rubber bands (producing circle designs)
- by rolling the fabric and tying it at different intervals (producing line designs)

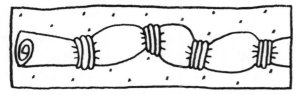

- by fan-folding the fabric and tying it at various intervals. The ties must be tight.

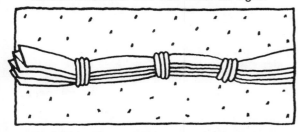

The fabric is immersed in dye, rinsed and hung to dry before removing the ties.
It is then ironed and can be redyed for further effect.
Use the batik method.

Batik

Heat batik wax in a frypan until it flows freely and is warm enough to be absorbed into the fabric.
Paint, drip or stamp the wax on to the fabric and allow it to dry. (The wax can be crumpled or cracked to create a crazed effect.)
Immerse the fabric into a cold-water dye and allow to dry.
Remove the wax by placing the fabric between sheets of absorbent paper and ironing with a moderate iron. Keep replacing the paper until the wax is removed.

Decorating with appliqué

The collage activities of the previous Phases (using fabric and thread glued to paper or cardboard) can be extended to appliqué work. Appliqué simply means sewing one cloth to another cloth—a stitched collage.

Fabric pieces can be stitched to a background using simple stitches. A three-dimensional effect can be obtained by padding, pleating, crumpling or rolling fabrics prior to attaching.

Decorative items such as old jewellery, shells, beads or buttons can also be added. Stitch with yarn or draw with felt-tip pens to add a linear quality to the design.

The designs for appliqué and other decorative work can be discussed during and following production of the piece through questions such as:

Does the design express an idea, a simple message, a feeling, a symbol, or tell a story?

What are the qualities of the design—the shapes, the colours and the textures?

Why is it important to keep the design simple and clear?

Which colours and shapes are the most expressive?

What materials and techniques did you use to create the design?

How do you think others will feel when they look at your design?

Fabric-making activities

The fabric-making techniques of knotting, weaving, plaiting and so on can be extended to include knitting and crochet.

The idea of knitting—of making a row of loops and interlocking another row—can be demonstrated by using a length of wood with nails hammered into it. Circular knitting using a cotton reel with nails hammered into it can also be used to demonstrate this.

Once the process has been understood more formal skills of casting on, casting off and plain knitting can be introduced.

Plain knitting

Put the point of the right-hand needle through the first stitch on the left-hand needle from the front to the back.

Wrap the wool between the two needles over the loop.

Bring the right-hand needle point back to front, pulling the wool through the old stitch to make a new stitch.

Pull the old stitch off the left-hand needle.

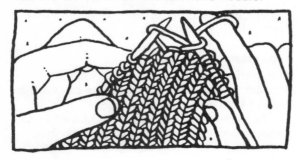

Crochet first with the fingers. Make a loop in a thread, pulling a second loop through the first, a third through the second and so on. Continue until a chain is made. Crochet in the same way using a hook. More formal stitches can then be introduced.

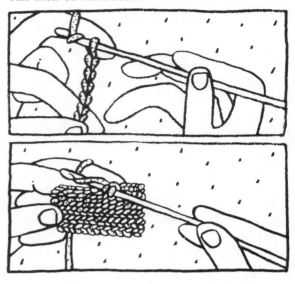

Chain stitch

Tie a loop of thread on the crochet hook.
Place a second thread loop on the thread finger.
Pass the hook under the thread on the finger and catch it with the hook.
Draw the thread through the loops.
Repeat and extend the chain to the desired length.

Crafting and Presenting

The children could use fabrics and threads:
- to appliqué banners, wall hangings, patchwork quilts, cushion covers, dolls and toys
- to stitch and appliqué imaginative objects and designs on clothing such as blue denim jeans or shirts. Add pieces of cloth, beads, buttons, braid or ricrac to complete the designs
- to weave, knot and stitch articles such as wall hangings, banners, a class mural made up of small individual pieces patched together
- to dye, using either tie-dye or batik techniques. Make bags, scarves, wall hangings, puppets' or dolls' clothes
- to knit or crochet belts, scarves, hats, bags, dolls, puppets' or dolls' clothes.

DRAWING
Phase 1

LEARNING OBJECTIVES

1 Children will be introduced to and explore the ideas of line, shape and marks.
2 Children will be introduced to a variety of drawing materials and discover the potential of them.
3 Children will draw on a variety of surfaces.
4 Children will discuss the content of their drawings and value their own and others' efforts.
5 Children will show a willingness to use drawings to express their ideas and to illustrate their thoughts through writing.
6 Children will become familiar with language relating to drawing: pencil, crayon, charcoal, pastel, texta, draw, marks, line (curved, straight, curled, thick, thin, wobbly, twisted, long, short), shape (circle, square, triangle, rectangle), marks (dots, flicks, smudges, rough, smooth, swirling, spinning), picture.

LEARNING EXPERIENCES

Getting Started

Introduce drawing materials
Provide the children with a variety of drawing materials, such as pencils, crayons, charcoal, pastels and felt-tipped pens. Allow them to explore the potential of these by drawing, scribbling, writing, colouring and making marks, lines and shapes.

Record the children's responses during these informal activities. Display them. Make charts like the one which follows.

WHAT YOU CAN DO WITH CRAYONS, PENCILS, CHARCOAL AND TEXTAS –
- smudge
- scribble
- scratch
- draw
- colour
- write
- rub
- mix-colours
- make lines- and shapes
- make marks

Draw in sand
Use hands to make marks, lines and shapes in the sandpit. Use also found tools such as sticks, stones and leaves.

Make lines and shapes
Use plasticine, sticks, pins, wool or string and make lines that: stand up, point downwards and upwards, run across one another, go round and round, go sideways, change direction, make shapes.

Ask the children to make lines with their bodies. Make: a long line, a short line, lines that meet in the middle, a curved line, a wriggly line.

Ask the children what happens when a line joins itself – it becomes a shape.

Record the children's discoveries on charts, posters, in books, on the chalkboard, anywhere.

LINES CAN BE –

- curved
- thick
- thin
- long
- short
- curled
- wriggly
- twisted
- straight

SHAPES CAN BE –

- circle
- flat
- round
- square
- triangle
- rectangle
- straight-sides
- curved-sides

MARKS CAN BE –

- dots
- spots
- rough
- hairy
- flicks
- smooth
- smudges
- spinning
- zig-zags
- crossed-spinning

WE CAN MAKE LINES, MARKS AND SHAPES WITH –

- sticks
- chalk
- pens
- stones
- twigs
- wire
- pencils
- crayons
- pastels
- matches
- charcoal
- ink pens
- threads
- our-bodies
- paper-strips
- ice-cream-sticks

WE CAN MAKE LINES, MARKS AND SHAPES ON –

- paper
- bark
- sand
- wood
- charts
- glass
- concrete
- material
- black-boards
- the ground

Developing Concepts and Techniques

The children's personal experiences are the main source of ideas for beginning artists. Ideas may be generated through class outings, drama, physical activity, dance and literature. Class or group brainstorming and discussion sessions also help to clarify ideas. Lists can provide resources for children to use in drawing.

The following questions will promote discussion and interest in drawing.

What is drawing?

What can you draw with?

What do you like to draw?

What do you like to draw with?

Is drawing the same as painting?

How are drawing and writing different?

Are drawing and colouring the same?

Where do we see drawings?

Can a drawing tell a story?

As in other areas of the art program, the choice of topic and of ideas for drawing should rest mainly with the artist. Techniques can be developed systematically through activities and discussion. The following drawing activities are helpful.

Use drawing materials

Make a long line with pastel.

Make a smudged mark with charcoal.

Make a line that changes direction with pencil.

Make a shape with smaller shapes inside it. Colour the shape using the pastel.

Decorate a line with charcoal marks.

Use the pencil to write with.

Colour with one colour and blend another over the top to make a new colour.

Make marks, lines and shapes

Use any drawing implement to make: swirling marks, spinning marks, dotted and spotted marks, straight lines, curved lines, smudged lines, round shapes, curved shapes, shapes with marks, lines in shapes.

Colour mixing activities

Make dots of one colour, make dots of another, hold it at a distance. Can you see a new colour?

Colour lightly with one colour, colour over the top with another. Did you make a new colour?

Draw squiggles of one colour, draw squiggles of another between them, hold it at a distance. Can you see another colour?

Discussion

Encourage the children to discuss their drawings or 'pictures' with others at various stages during the process. Drawings can be enlarged (using an overhead projector) to highlight aspects. Discussion should centre firstly on content and then draw attention to techniques used. Sharing time may proceed as follows.

Tell us about your picture.

Does it tell a story?

Questions may be asked to clarify content.

What is this part?

Why is this figure larger?

Which part do you like?

Tell us more about what you did there?

Techniques can then be highlighted through questioning.

How did you make this mark?

What do these marks remind you of?

This is a long line; how did you make it so wobbly?

What is this curved shape?

Could you make it again?

Crafting and Presenting

The children could draw:
- using crayons, pencils, pastels, charcoal and felt-tipped pens
- to illustrate a story before or after writing
- pictures in sequence to illustrate an event or a story
- using a mark, line or shape as a starter for a picture
- using marks, lines and shapes to add detail to a picture
- to decorate a clay or plasticene model.

DRAWING
Phase 2

LEARNING OBJECTIVES

1 Children will explore the techniques of creating line, shape, marks and colour through a variety of drawing materials.
2 Children will draw and modify shapes and symbols in their pictures.
3 Children will use drawings to express their ideas and feelings and record experiences and observations.
4 Children will produce a drawing that can be shared and discussed with others.
5 Children will revise and refine a drawing to illustrate ideas to others.
6 Children will become familiar with language relating to drawing: twirl, twist, drag, roll, swirl, stamp, pull, flick, pattern, symbol, rubbings, detail, decorate, dark, light, shade, overlapping, sign.

LEARNING EXPERIENCES

Getting Started

Observe lines and shapes

Examine collections of objects or photographs of objects to observe lines, marks and shapes.
Rounded shapes: shells, balls, pine cones, pebbles
Rectangular shapes; windows, doors, buildings, boxes
Triangular shapes: trees, roofs
Irregular shapes: clouds, figures, cars
Scaley patterns: on fish, reptiles
Straight lines: telephone wires, lines on tennis courts
Marks that make patterns: brickwork, wire netting
Observe lines, marks and shapes in the immediate environment. Classify and record these: curved shapes in the school yard, straight lines in our street, marks we saw on the ground on our walk, patterns in our school yard, signs around us.

Make rubbings

Make rubbings of various natural and man-made objects to discover line, shape and texture (bricks, grass, leaves, coins, buttons, cement, gravel, torn or cut-out pieces of card, sand, lace, hessian, loops of string).
Record these for future reference as some may be useful as starters for drawings or to add detail in a drawing.

Experiment with drawing materials

Experiment with a variety of drawing materials (pencil, pastel, charcoal, crayon, texta) to make marks, lines and shapes.
Discuss the different effects produced by using the end, the side, the tip, the corner of a drawing implement.
Fully explore the use of each material—by twirling, twisting, dragging, rolling, swirling, stamping, pulling, flicking.

Look at different representations

Observe the many ways objects are represented in drawings by classroom artists. Record these.

HOW WE DRAW TREES —

HOW WE DRAW THE SUN —

HOW WE DRAW PEOPLE —

Draw a line.

Draw it again and make it hop, skip and jump.

Make it jump up and fall down.

Can you make it look as if it moves?

Developing Concepts and Techniques

Previously learned techniques can be applied to new activities in drawing.

Start with lines and marks

Encourage the children to refer to the charts of marks, lines and shapes made with the various materials and to use these in their pictures. A mark, for example, may be selected to provide a starter for a piece. Other marks, shapes or lines may be used to add details or special features to a picture.

Discuss the use of marks, lines and shapes before, during and after making pictures.

What do these marks look like?

How could you describe them?

Where have you seen a mark like this?

What could they be used for?

Does this line look like something to you?

Could you use it in a picture?

How did you make that shape?

What part of the pencil did you use to make this mark?

Modify shapes and symbols

Encourage the children to add to or change a shape or symbol, initially by directed activities.

Make a circle.

Make as many different circles as you can.

Change the circles by adding lines or marks.

Discussion

Discussion of the children's drawing or pictures will lead to revision and refinement.

Sharing time during the process may proceed through questions such as:

What is your picture about?

What is this part?

Can you explain this bit to me?

Can you tell me more about this part?

Is there anything you could add in this picture?

Are there any marks that would add detail to this part?

Is there anything you could change?

An overhead projector is a useful aid when revising or refining drawings together in a small group or as a class.

Crafting and Presenting

The children could draw:

• using a variety of drawing implements such as crayons, pencils, pastels, charcoal and felt-tipped pens

• using marks, lines and shapes to revise and refine a drawing

• to decorate models

• to illustrate personal writing

• to illustrate a story sequence

• as an aid to research

• simple maps or plans.

DRAWING
Phase 3

LEARNING OBJECTIVES

1 Children will use a variety of materials and techniques in their drawings.
2 Children will use a combination of materials and techniques.
3 Children will observe and draw objects (and people) from different points of view.
4 Children will use line and marks to create texture and detail in a drawing.
5 Children will use line, shapes and marks to express moods and feelings in a drawing.
6 Children will use drawings to express their ideas and feelings, to record observations and as an aid to research.
7 Children will become familiar with language relating to drawing: figure, map, plan, diagram, sketch, technique, Surrealism, abstract, background, foreground, highlight, focus, exhibit, tone, texture, feelings, emotions.

LEARNING EXPERIENCES

Getting Started

Examine line, shape and pattern

Use a display of pictures and photographs to stimulate interest and discussion of line, shape and pattern in natural and man-made things.

Observe lines, shapes and patterns where they occur in nature; for example, the lines in a snail's shell, on sea shells, spider's webs, raindrops running down a window pane, rolling hills, the veins in leaves.

Observe, too, the lines in man-made structures; for example, telephone wires, wire netting, tall buildings, fences, bridges.

Use the overhead projector to observe the line and shape of natural and man-made

objects. Place them on the top and project the images on the screen or wall. You could trace the images.

Different viewpoints

Look at objects from different points of view—from the top, side, back, front, underneath, up close, far away, focusing on one part only.

Make rubbings

Make rubbings of various natural and man-made objects to observe marks and patterns. Record these marks as resources for picture-making.

Observe moving objects

Look at films or provide direct experiences to observe the line and direction of moving objects; for example, a leaping kangaroo, dancers, a tennis ball during a game.

Collect and discuss pictures of people using their bodies in different ways. Discuss how people use their arms and legs when moving.

What shapes can you see?

Are the arms and legs stretched?

Are the bodies curved and twisted?

Record the children's vocabulary for describing movements: stretch, arch, twist, flick, sharp turn, flexible, curve, quick.

Observe children at play or people involved in sporting activity.

Discuss body movements and facial expressions.

How do you feel when you are winning?

How do you feel when you are losing?

How are the faces different?

What happens to our mouths? eyes?

Visit a gallery to view exhibits

Draw moods

Use lines, marks and shapes to express moods and feelings.

Make a line, shape or mark that is: happy, lazy or tired, surprised, angry, goes up a hill and runs all the way down.

Make lines, shapes and marks that you like/dislike.

Combine lines, shapes and marks to tell a story about: a clown's face, a sad face, a grumpy face, a frightened face.

Draw people in different situations

For example, draw people: in the snow, inside a machine, in the sea, on a bicycle, under a car.

Draw movement

Draw a person in as many different ways as possible; for example, while playing a sport — running, jumping, kicking, catching, falling.

Discussion

Encourage the children to discuss their ideas, and the techniques they used to present them, through questions such as:

What is your drawing/picture about?

What is the focal point of this piece? Why?

How have you highlighted this?

How do you think the audience will feel when they look at your picture?

Is there a part that you particularly like?

Is there any part you could change?

Did you use any particular marks, lines or shapes to give the audience this feeling?

Developing Concepts and Techniques

The children need time and materials to experiment with lines, marks, shapes and composition to develop ideas before and during the process of drawing. They need time and space to complete quick sketches, try marks and patterns, make a rubbing to check the texture of something or complete a quick composition sketch. They will begin to make choices concerning methods and ideas and will be more eager to experiment during the process. It is important, therefore, that value is placed on these efforts and that children be given time to experiment without having to produce a final product.

The following activities will encourage this experimentation.

Draw objects from different points of view

Draw from the top, side, back, front, underneath, up close, far away, to show only part of the object.

Can you show me the inside as well as the outside of your cubby?

Can you draw your car from the top?

Can you draw your model aeroplane from the front?

Can you draw your friend from the side/front/back?

Add detail

Use lines, marks and rubbings to create texture and add detail to an object.

Can you use feathery marks to add detail to your sketch of a bird?

Can you use a mark as a starting point in a picture?

Can you use a rubbing as the background to your picture?

Practise lines of marks that look like: grass, water, the sky, the earth.

Make marks, lines and shapes for use in 'making' people. Look at these and relate them to parts of people.

Did you use techniques to add detail to your drawing?

Did you change or modify your drawing along the way? Where? How?

Crafting and Presenting

The children could draw:
- using a variety of materials and techniques
- using combinations of materials and techniques; for example, pastel and ink

Pastel and ink drawing

Cover the page with bright, heavy areas of crayon or oil pastel colour.
Paint over this with Indian ink or black paint.
Scratch back a drawing using the end of a knife, a nail or any sharp implement.

or

Apply a wash of ink, food dye or thin paint before or after drawing with pastel—as a means of creating a background or as a cover over existing drawings. Interesting effects can be achieved by blending two colours.

- by combining marks, lines and shapes to create symbols or logos
- by repeating marks, lines and shapes to design patterns or to decorate
- to illustrate personal writing and to record experiences and observations; for example, a series of actions in a sporting book
- as an aid to a research project
- for a classroom newspaper; include lettering, drawing, comic strips and so on
- a poster, billboard or sign
- using a particular style; for example, a Surrealist or abstract drawing.

DRAWING
Phase 4

LEARNING OBJECTIVES

1 Children will review and refine concepts of line, shape and marks through drawing with a wide variety of materials.
2 Children will use the techniques of perspective and shading.
3 Children will sketch from still-life and real-life situations.
4 Children will compose, develop and complete a drawing that can be presented to an audience for discussion.
5 Children will refine their skills of figure drawing.
6 Children will become familiar with language relating to drawing: outline, pose, composition, balance, focal point, still life, horizon, skyline, illustrate, lettering, logo, symbol, perspective, vanishing point, shade, tone, texture, cartoon.

LEARNING EXPERIENCES

Getting Started

Discuss other artists' works
Use a display of drawings and sketches to stimulate interest and discussion and to highlight different artists' techniques of making line, shape, marks and colour.

What is this picture about?
How do you feel when you look at it?
Is it realistic?
What drawing media did he/she use?
Do you think the material used suits the subject matter?
Why?
Has the artist used certain lines and marks in the picture?

Are some marks, shapes or lines repeated?

Point out examples of shading in the works of artists like Rembrandt and Giorgio De Chirico. (De Chirico used long, end-of-the-day shadows of buildings, anonymous figures in the distance, and, in general, a great deal of personal symbolism.)

Look at Aboriginal art
Look at the use of line and marks in the functional and decorative art work of the Australian Aborigines or of other native cultures. Observe the importance of line, shape, marks, shades and patterns.

Visit an art gallery

Look at writing and signs
Discover decorative writing in the environment; for example, on birthday cakes, neon signs.
Collect and discuss examples of writing from other cultures and times.
Look at how line is used in symbols, road signs, billboards, logos, monograms.

Examine objects in detail
Look carefully at objects with one eye closed and very close up. Do not touch the objects or move them in any way. Look for lines or marks. Look for shadows and reflections.
Look carefully at your hands, arms, legs with one eye closed and very close up. Look for spots, wrinkles, colours or reflections.
Look at a friend's face very carefully.

Is he/she happy, sad, excited, bored?
How can you tell?
Are there any marks on your friend's face?
Are there any shadows?
Is one eye different from the other?

Are there any reflections on your friend's face?

Look at a scene in detail

Look down the end of the street.

Does the end of the street look wide or narrow?

Can you see as many things at the end of the street as you can near where you stand?

Are there any signs? Can you see anything shining brightly?

Is anything overlapping?

Are there any textured areas?

Observe people in action

Children can demonstrate actions such as skateboarding, roller skating, kicking a football and riding a bike, as others watch and notice the shapes made with their bodies—how they bend, move, twist and curl. Take photos of children in action poses. Observe also facial expressions and mannerisms.

Invisible drawing

Draw with lemon juice using a thin brush or pen and nib. Iron over this and the drawing will appear like magic.

Draw with a white candle on white paper. Brush over this with thin, coloured ink or paint to reveal the picture.

Developing Concepts and Techniques

Children in this Phase must be guided towards independence. True independence involves the ability to make judgements and decisions about the content, form and likely communicative effectiveness of drawings. Teachers must provide a wealth of ideas and experiences to allow for this.

Painting, drawing and print-making should not be identified only with 'picture making'. There are many ways that children can use these concepts and techniques across the curriculum. The ideas listed in the Crafting and Presenting section provide choices for children.

The following activities will help to develop techniques.

Use perspective in a drawing

Make a drawing in pastel or crayon that shows that some things seem close while others are far away. Include detail in the foreground and draw things as they appear; for example, buildings with rusty spoutings and broken windows, cars with shiny hubcaps.

Work out models for children to use such as:

Lightly sketch in the horizon line.

Decide on a vanishing point(s), a point where all lines will meet.

Draw some guide lines to the vanishing point(s).

Sketch the basic shapes of buildings, trees, power poles, using the guide lines. Begin in the background.

Highlight their success by questioning.

Which objects are the furtherest away?

Where does your picture lead us?

What is in the middleground and the foreground of your picture?

How did you highlight the things in the foreground?

Use shading and shadow

In learning how to draw, one fundamental skill is the ability to use shading to create volume or three dimensions. Charcoal is an excellent medium for creating tones and shading as it enables the artist not only to make black, but also to get many variations of grey in between.

Show the works of other artists and point out examples of shading in their pictures. Explain how tones and shades are used to create moods in a picture.

Demonstrate some shading techniques.

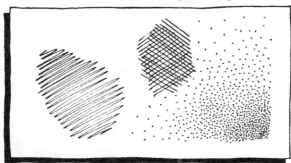

To highlight the effects of light and shadow, create a single source of light using a torch, spotlight or reading lamp.

Still-life drawing

Still-life drawing allows the children to practise and develop their skills in composition, shading and texture.

Look at the works of artists such as Henri Matisse, Paul Cézanne, Georges Braque, William Harnett and Charles W. Peale.

Still-life arrangements may include: toys, model cars, dolls, machinery, fruit, glassware, musical instruments, antique items, skulls, candles, clocks and flowers.

Provide models for the children to follow such as:

Lightly draw the main lines of the objects to develop your composition.

Emphasize variety by keeping some forms larger than others.

Do not make your arrangement too complicated.

Look carefully for light and shades, and block in the main areas.

In discussion, highlight the many possible interpretations of the still life by questions such as:

From your position what have you chosen to be the focal point?

How did you position the pieces in the picture space?

How did you decide on the colour combinations?

Do you think the picture is balanced?

What techniques did you use to create shading and texture?

Could you have begun in a different way?

Could you have completed the picture from a different point of view, perhaps to appeal to a different audience?

Is there part of the arrangement you would like to draw or paint again?

Sketch figures from real life

Use a real-life situation such as a sporting event or use action photographs for figure drawing. To begin, make quick sketches to suggest the pose only. Vary the poses as much as possible. Then encourage some detail by questioning.

Who is your person?

Where is he/she?

What is he/she doing?

What is he/she wearing?

What is her/his facial expression? Why?

Encourage the children to look carefully for light and shade, and simplification of shapes, feelings, expressions and effects.

Use Surrealist subject matter

Surrealism refers to the world of dreams, the subconscious and the imagination. It allows you to go beyond the bounds of reality for your subject matter, emphasizing a more inventive exploration of visual relationships.

Look at the works of artists such as René Magritte, Giorgio De Chirico and Salvador Dali.

Good subject matter includes caskets, skulls, mythical creatures, spider's webs, castles, strange light sources and eerie shadows.

Crafting and Presenting

The children could draw:
- using a variety of materials and techniques
- to illustrate personal writing
- to illustrate pamphlets, book jackets, brochures, record covers, reports, advertisements, posters, postcards, newspapers, greeting cards, charts
- outdoor objects or figures
- using a particular subject matter or style; for example, a still life, Surrealism
- to illustrate current events as an artist may do for a newspaper or magazine; for example, courtroom drama

63

- to illustrate impressions from drama, music, physical activity
- using type and calligraphy to design: posters in various writing styles, monograms, logos, simple diagrams, graphic symbols, lettering books, coats-of-arms, school notice boards and displays

- cartoons and comic strips
- as an aid to research across curriculum areas.

PRINT-MAKING
Phase 1

LEARNING OBJECTIVES

1 Children will be introduced to the idea of making a 'print'.
2 Children will explore and discover 'printing' using a variety of found objects (natural and man-made).
3 Children will be introduced to the idea of 'pattern' as a repetitive image.
4 Children will learn the techniques of making prints by rolling, stamping and rubbing.
5 Children will become familiar with language relating to print-making: print, printing, fold, press, mirror, footprint, hand print, fingerprint, texture, surface, rubbing, rolling, stamping, repeat, pattern.

LEARNING EXPERIENCES

Getting Started

Look at design in nature
The children look at a collection of natural objects and pictures of objects to observe nature's design; for example, spiral designs on shells, veins in leaves, markings on animals, patterns on the bark of trees and so on. Make rubbings of these, where possible, or press them into wet sand to see the 'print' they leave.

Make a record of a class walk
Take the children for a walk to a nearby park or creek or around the school grounds. Take some thin paper, plus pastels, charcoal or thick pencils. Make rubbings of the different textures along the way. On returning to the school cut out the rubbings, paste them together on a large sheet of paper, then connect them with lines. You will have a visual record of your walk.

Discuss the different lines in the rubbings: thick, thin, long, straight, curved, wiggly, zigzagged, heavy, light.
Discuss the textures: rough, smooth, heavy, light, fine, coarse. Record these for future reference.

Make prints
Make foot and shoe prints in the sandpit or sand tray. You could make a pattern in the sand using different foot prints, hand prints or prints of other body parts.
Make thumb, finger and hand prints by the following method. Pour paint on to a board, use a roller to spread the paint evenly over the board, place a hand/finger on the board, transfer to paper. Record these on a chart.

Decorate thumb prints
Make 'thumbody' or 'thumbthing' by using a pencil or felt pen to add features to a thumb print.

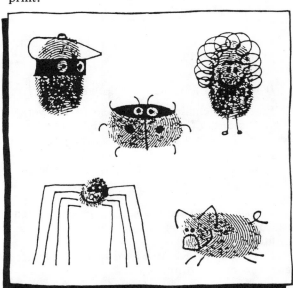

Make a mirror print

Paint on one half of the paper, fold and press lightly. The print will be reproduced on the other half.

Use found objects to print

Use natural materials like leaves, twigs, pebbles, gum nuts, flowers, or man-made materials like corks, paper clips, pegs to make a print.

Highlight the effects gained by questioning.

Which objects did you use?

Can you match the object with its print?

Can you use many parts of the same object to print?

Can you change a print?

What does this print look like?

Which print do you like the best?

How could you use it in a picture?

Introduce the idea of pattern

Use wrapping paper or printed fabric to demonstrate that patterns are a repetitive image. Use a variety of materials to create a pattern (horizontal, vertical or circular).

Developing Concepts and Techniques

Through class and group discussions lead the children to understand the ways printing can be used to create patterns and pictures.

Questioning may proceed as follows:

What is printing?

What can we print with?

How can we use a print (to make a pattern, to make a picture)?

Where do we see prints?

If we repeat a print, what do we make?

For young children who are struggling with the techniques of print-making, the content or ideas behind the piece may be secondary.

Introduce a variety of simple printing methods

Soak string in paint and pull it between two pieces of paper.

Cut, press or twist the surface of corrugated cardboard, apply paint to the surface and print.

Incise the surface of a hard block of clay, apply paint and print.

Roll a piece of clay into the shape of a car tyre, place a skewer through the middle, incise the circumference of the clay, apply paint and roll it on to the paper.

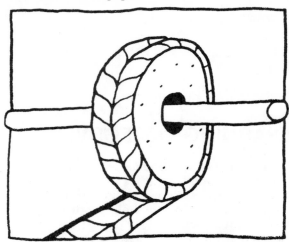

Dribble or paint PVA in a controlled pattern on to stiff cardboard and allow to dry. This may be used for printing.

Colour-mixing activities

Print with one colour, then print over the top with another to discover a new colour.

Blob two colours on to a board, blend just a little leaving some of the original colours. Print to reveal the shades and colours. Add another colour and repeat the process.

Create a pattern

Print using objects and colours to create a pattern. For example, you could use two objects and two colours; alternate colour and object.

Discussion

Encourage the children to discuss their prints or pictures with others at various stages during the process. Through helpful discussion, techniques can be refined, effects highlighted and meaning enhanced.

Tell us about your print/picture.

Does your print/picture tell a story?

Does you print have a title?

Which part do you like the best?

Invite the other children to tell the artist what is good about the print or which part is best.

Tell us more about this part here.
How did you make this print?
What colours did you use?
What objects did you use?
What part of the object did you use?
Could you use it in a different way?
Is there a pattern in your picture?
How did you make the pattern?

Crafting and Presenting

The children could print:
- using a variety of natural and man-made objects
- to illustrate a story before or after writing
- to make a pattern with shapes and colours
- using specified techniques; for example, a continuous pattern by using a roll of clay, a picture using corrugated card to stamp print in several colours
- to make a picture using prints made using a variety of methods. Prints that are successful in suggesting shape and texture can be selected from the 'tries' and added to the picture
- to decorate or pattern a place mat, a model, a book cover, a card or a construction.

PRINT-MAKING
Phase 2

LEARNING OBJECTIVES

1 Children will print with a variety of natural and man-made objects.
2 Children will make their own objects to use in printing.
3 Children will add to or change a print as they modify and refine their ideas.
4 Children will use a variety of pattern-making techniques.
5 Children will learn the techniques of mono-printing.
6 Children will share and discuss their efforts with others.
7 Children will become familiar with language relating to print-making: natural, man-made, reproduce, repeating, roller, arrange, design, pattern, variety, shapes, position, mono-printing, overlap, focus, image.

LEARNING EXPERIENCES

Getting Started

Collect printing materials

Collect materials that may be suitable for stamped or rolled prints. Go for a walk along a creek, in a park or in the school ground to collect objects. Discuss the basis of selection; for example, shape, texture, line and the likely effects the objects will produce.

Which object(s) has an interesting shape?
Feel the surfaces of the objects. Which do you think will produce the best print?

Experiment with printing materials

Experiment with a variety of natural and man-made objects to print with (stamped prints).

Discuss the different effects produced by using the end, the side, the tip, the front, the back of the objects.

Explore the use of the objects and record the effects in books, on posters and charts.

These records can be used for future reference in picture-making sessions.

Make rubbings

Examine collections of objects, feel the texture and discuss the shapes, lines and marks on the surfaces. Make rubbings of various objects. Cut and paste these on to charts for reference during other sessions.

Make patterns

Incorporate a variety of pattern-making activities as quick, problem-solving experiences. They may include: repeating a print at regular or varied intervals, changing the size of a print and repeating it, repeating a print in a band around something, repeating a print in an overall pattern, changing the colour of a print while repeating it, making a pattern using one colour and two shapes, making a pattern using one shape and two colours, making a finger painting and taking a print from it, printing a dominant figure with subordinate figures around it, overlapping one print with another using a different colour.

Change prints

Encourage the children to add to or change a print. Make a single print. Then change it by: drawing or painting, printing over, adding other prints to it, adding a print with another colour, overlapping with a series of prints.

Group or class sessions will give the children ideas for revising and refining their own prints.

'Find the print'

Hide a print amongst other prints by using a different object.

Developing Concepts and Techniques

The following experiences are designed to build on the methods and ideas developed in Phase 1.

Encourage the children to refer to the charts of prints made by stamping, rolling or rubbing. They can use ideas from these charts in their pictures. A print may be selected to provide a starter for a picture or painting or, alternatively, prints may be used to add detail to a picture or painting. A print can also be used as the focal point of a picture.

Discuss the many ways a single object can be used to make prints.

Encourage young artists to take chances with the methods of printing. Provide them with scrap paper to 'try' a print before committing it to the picture. Make certain these 'tries' are valued and discussed or kept for future reference.

Print with made objects

Allow children to make their own objects to print with. These can be created by:
- cutting shapes from vegetables
- building up the surface of cardboard by gluing fabric, string, matches or found objects to the surface
- gluing string, fabrics, paper, rubber bands, feathers, leaves, ribbon to the outside surface of a tin or bottle. Roll this into paint and then on to paper to make a continuous print.

Use the process of mono-printing

This involves rolling out paint on to the work surface and taking a direct print by pressing paper down on to the surface after it has been worked. The surface can be worked in a variety of ways; for example, by drawing, by laying things on to it.

Mono-printing is a spontaneous and exciting process that gives an instant, direct and unexpected print.

Variations to the process include:
- drawing on the back of the paper with a pen, stick, pencil or fingernail
- pressing found objects—buttons, wood scraps, cardboard, plastic shapes—into the back of the paper. Peel the paper off carefully
- tearing or cutting paper shapes, and placing them on the painted surface. Place the paper carefully on top and draw or press on to the back of the sheet
- mixing a variety of colours on to the flat surface to produce a multi-coloured mono-print
- carefully placing string, ribbon, thread, open-weave fabrics or leaves on to the painted surface, placing the paper on top, and then drawing on the paper.

Discussion

Discussion of the children's pictures created using prints will lead to revision and refinement. Sharing time may proceed through questions such as:

What is your picture about?
What is this part?

Can you tell me more about this part?
Is there any part you would like to change?
How can you change it (by printing over the top, by adding another print)?

Be careful not to insist on change. Children need to learn to know when not to revise or change.

Would you like to add anything?
Can anyone suggest where something could be added?
Is there any part that could be used in another picture?
What would you like to do with your print now (display it, use it as the cover of a book, write a story about it)?

Crafting and Presenting

The children could print:
- using a variety of found objects (natural and man-made)
- using made objects to create a picture (rolled, stamped, rubbed, mono-printed)
- to make posters and cards
- to create patterns for book covers, wrapping paper, cards
- a group mural using all the print-making methods tried.

PRINT-MAKING
Phase 3

LEARNING OBJECTIVES

1 Children will collect, make and select objects to use in printing.
2 Children will make choices concerning materials and techniques.
3 Children will use a combination of materials and techniques.
4 Children will use printing for a variety of purposes; for example, establishing a background, creating a focal point.
5 Children will practise the additive, subtractive and transferring methods of printing.
6 Children will learn the technique of stencilling.
7 Children will become familar with language relating to print-making: display, decorate, print board, pressure, multi-coloured, composition, focal point, additive, subtractive, transferring, stencil, pre-cut, technique.

LEARNING EXPERIENCES

Getting Started

Look at line, shape, texture and pattern

Use a display of pictures and photographs to stimulate interest in and discussion of line, shape, texture and pattern in natural and man-made things.

Observe pattern where it occurs in nature; for example, in the scales on a fish, veins in leaves, animal prints in the sand, the path a snake makes as it moves along, sand blown by wind.

Observe, too, the pattern in man-made things; for example, fabric patterns, patterns on posters and banners, decoration on ceramic pots, patterns of decorative markings on kitchen objects.

Encourage the children to bring along patterned objects to look at the designs and colours used.

Collect printing materials

The children can sort and select materials that are suitable for use in the various printing methods; for example, leaves for stamping and stencilling, magazine cut-outs for stencilling, string for mono-printing.

'Quick' printing

Experiment with collected and made objects in quick activities to 'try' a print. Discuss the effects gained.

Tell us about this print?
Does this print remind you of anything?
What did you use to make this mark?
How did you use it?
Could this print be used in a picture?
Can you add to or change the print in any way?
Did you improve it?
Which print do you think is the best? Why?

Developing Concepts and Techniques

The children need time and materials to experiment with the various methods of print-making. Prints can be made quickly on scrap paper and the effect discussed. The best effects can be cut out and filed or charted for easy reference.

Ideas to encourage experimentation

Create prints that look like: grass, storm clouds, bricks, foliage and so on.

Create a single print and then establish the meaning through questioning.

What could it be?

What can you turn it into?

Where is it?

Use a print to add texture to a painting or drawing.

Where could you add texture?

What could you use?

How could you make that print?

Use a print pattern as the background to a picture.

What does the print pattern remind you of?

What could it be?

What could be in the picture with this background?

Refine the techniques of mono-printing

Try the following variations.

Additive method

Paint a picture on to a printing board (sheet of glass, lino or laminex square).
Paint may be applied using brushes, a sponge, fingers, a toothbrush.

Place a sheet of paper over the board and rub evenly.

Lift the paper off the board.

Subtractive method

Apply an even coating of paint to a printing surface with a roller.
Create a picture by taking paint off the surface. To remove the paint, use fingers, a sponge, brushes and so on.
Place paper over the board, apply pressure and lift.

Transferring method

Apply an even coating of paint to a printing board with a sponge or roller.
Gently drop the paper on to the board. Do not apply pressure.
Using a pencil or the end of a paint brush draw a picture on the paper.
Lift the paper.

Multi-coloured mono-printing produces striking effects.

Stencilling

Making a print using a stencil is simple and the process allows children to experiment before completing a picture. The composition can easily be changed as the stencils are re-arranged on the page.

Stencils are placed on paper. The children draw or rub from the stencil out, on to the paper, to create an image using pencils, pastels, chalk, crayons, textas, charcoal or paint. Rollers and toothbrushes can be used to apply paint around a stencil.

through questions such as:

> What is your picture about?
> Is there a focal point?
> How did you create the focal point?
> What printing technique(s) did you use?
> Did you repeat a print for a special effect such as a background?
> How do you think the audience will feel when they look at your picture?
> What printing objects did you use?

Crafting and Presenting

The children could print:

- using a variety of materials and methods to make a picture, to decorate
- using a variety of techniques for particular purposes; for example to establish a background in a picture, to add texture to a painting
- using a stencil to create a T-shirt design
- to make a print book showing the techniques, patterns and effects created by different objects. The prints may become writing starters for personal imaginative pieces
- to make a poster or card
- using a variety of techniques to create an advertising billboard (small-group activity).

Discussion

Encourage the children to discuss their ideas, and the techniques they used to present them,

PRINT-MAKING
Phase 4

LEARNING OBJECTIVES

1 Children will review and refine a variety of print- and pattern-making techniques.
2 Children will select the most suitable printing techniques for a specified purpose.
3 Children will compose, develop and complete a picture using a combination of printing techniques and present it to an audience.
4 Children will learn a range of incised methods of print-making.
5 Children will become familiar with language relating to print-making: silk-screen, incised technique, incising, billboard, batik, lino-cut, polystyrene, indenting, relief process.

LEARNING EXPERIENCES

Getting Started

Discuss printed products

Use a display of pieces showing various printing techniques to stimulate interest and discussion. The display may include items such as: newspapers, magazines, screen-printed T-shirts, monograms, logos, posters, stencilled pictures or fabrics, batik prints.

Discussion can centre around details such as composition, design, simplicity of colour, sharpness of line and so on.

Look at art prints

Prints of original sketches or paintings can be displayed and discussed.

What is the difference between an original and a print?

Why do artists make prints of their works?

What is the value of the print in relation to the original?

Where do you see original art works?
Where do you see a print?

'Quick' printing

Introduce a variety of print- and pattern-making experiences as quick, problem-solving experiences. These will provide practice in previously learned methods. These experiences may include: using various stamped prints to make an overall pattern, combining stamped prints and mono-prints, using mono-prints as a background for a stencil.

Developing Concepts and Techniques

Children in this Phase should be encouraged to use and refine the wide variety of printing techniques experienced in the earlier Phases. They can make choices concerning the most useful method to suit the ideas being presented in a piece. Children may also be introduced to more advanced methods of print-making.

The incised method

There are now many opportunities for image-making using the incised method. Children were once restricted to the more difficult processes of lino-cut and wood-block printing, but the availability of soft working surfaces such as polystyrene, plastic and wax now make it possible for incising to be achieved simply by pushing a blunt cutting tool into the material, or by pressing or indenting the surface with a variety of simple tools. This makes the incised process much safer and simpler.

Incised polystyrene print-making
Draw a picture with biro on to a polystyrene tray.
Make sure the tray is flat and then apply paint using a roller.

Place the tray face down on to paper and press evenly.
Lift to reveal the print.

or

Heat a nail and burn a pattern or picture into a polystyrene block.
When the cutting is complete, apply paint to the block using a roller.
Stamp on to the paper.

or

Instead of polystyrene you can use corrugated card or materials such as corks or vegetables
Cut out a pattern using a sharp object.
Soak a sponge with paint.
Sit the paint-soaked sponge on a tray for convenience.
The stamps can be pressed into the sponge and printed on to the paper.

Lino-printing

Stress the need for careful planning before cutting and encourage the children to draw the desired picture or pattern on to the lino. They then cut areas of the lino using lino tools. The paint is rolled on or applied lightly with a brush or sponge, then a print is taken.

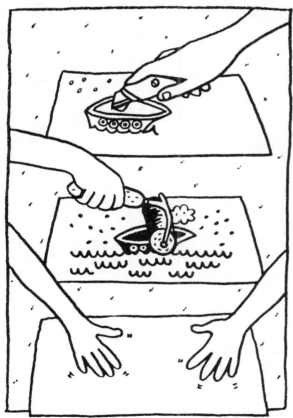

Use relief

Relief surfaces can be produced by building up (as well as cutting into) a material. Discuss the use of relief in old methods of typesetting for newspapers, posters and magazines.

Surfaces can be built up by gluing rubber bands, string, fabric pieces or pieces of card to wood blocks using PVA. The surfaces are inked and used for printing.

Other printing methods

More elaborate methods of printing such as screen-printing can be attempted by some students.

Discussion

As children develop their skills with the various printing techniques they can experiment with variations and combinations to produce their own prints and print styles. They can experiment with 'print tries', discuss the ideas and effects gained, and use them in their printed pieces. Encourage them to discuss how a piece will develop, to build on their strengths and to decide on the best direction to take to reach a final piece.

The teacher's role is to offer encouragement and support to guide the children gently towards a process of continuous self-examination.

Questioning through the process can proceed like this:

What am I trying to do in this piece?
What will my piece be about?
Do I need to try some ideas prior to committing them to my piece?
What print methods can I use?

Will I use a single print technique or repeated designs?

What materials do I need?

Which part is showing the most promise?

How can I build on this?

What is the best part?

As prints are added to the piece, children can discuss their partially completed or completed work with others. This leads to further self-examination.

What do the others think of my piece?

Could I have used a different method?

Did I create the best effect I could?

How does this compare with other pieces?

Crafting and Presenting

The children could print:

- using colour, shape and line to express moods and feelings
- to design posters, cards and billboards
- using combinations of techniques and colours
- on a variety of surfaces; for example, board, fabric
- to decorate book covers, cards, constructions, clay models, stationery
- in the production of a class or school newsletter or newspaper
- individual seals cut from cork or rubber to personalize notepaper or art work.

CONSTRUCTION
Phase 1

LEARNING OBJECTIVES

1 Children will be introduced to the idea of 'construction' and three-dimensional form.
2 Children will explore and discover the potential of paper and cardboard as construction materials.
3 Children will learn construction techniques including cutting, folding and joining with paper and cardboard.
4 Children will construct a model to illustrate an idea or a story.
5 Children will show a willingness to discuss their structures with others.
6 Children will become familiar with language relating to construction: crush, curl, staple, fold, pleat, fringe, glue, paste, roll, join, combine, reshape, cardboard, boxes, cartons, building, statue, steel, glass, metal, wood, concrete, scissors, cellotape, masking tape, puppet, mask, model, space.

LEARNING EXPERIENCES

Getting Started

Children become familiar with paper as one of their earliest experiences. Although they may never have thought of using it as a sculptural material, children will quickly learn that various kinds of papers can be used in various processes to produce different effects.

Experiment with paper

Provide the children with a variety of types of paper and allow them to explore how they can be transformed. Use available paper types such as: aluminium foil, butcher's paper, cellophane, cardboard, confetti, corrugated paper and card, gift-wrap paper, magazine paper, newsprint, paper bags, paper handkerchiefs, paper napkins, paper plates, paper towelling, tissue paper, wallpaper, waxed paper.

Encourage the children to relate their experiences to each other by grouping them in small groups. Record their discoveries.

WHAT WE CAN DO WITH PAPER -
- crush
- paste
- curl
- glue
- roll
- fold
- pleat
- staple
- fringe
- cut into - strips
- tear into - shapes

PAPER IS -
- rough
- dull
- thick
- thin
- smooth
- bright
- spongy
- shiny
- colourful
- textured
- see - through

Construct 'environments'

Provide the children with large sheets of cardboard, cardboard boxes, pieces of wood, polystyrene and paper which they can use to construct environments in the classroom. Spaces can be constructed for reading/writing corners, as sets for drama, or just as a space for quiet talk. The areas can be constantly changed, taken apart and added to.

Constructions can also be used to create areas such as: a shop, a post office, a dolls' corner, a quiet writing place such as a small hut, or an area related to a classroom theme.

Body 'constructions'

Ask the children to 'construct' with their bodies. Individually or in small groups the children can become 'a building', 'a statue', 'a bridge', 'a sculpture'.

Look at constructions

Go for a walk around the neighbourhood to observe the man-made constructions. List and then group and label the constructions according to common elements: bridge, statue, monument, building, pier, grave headstone, phone box, letter box, playground equipment. The children can draw some of these.

Discuss the materials used in the constructions (steel, glass, wood, metal, bricks, concrete). Record these on charts.

Developing Concepts and Techniques

The children's personal experiences are the main source of ideas for construction. Through observation and discussion of man-made structures the children get ideas about content and methods of building.

> What can you build or make?
>
> What can we build with?
>
> How is something you build different from a picture? (You can see all around.)
>
> What is a sculpture or statue?
>
> What is construction?

Introduce construction materials gradually through the various Phases as the children master techniques and concepts. In this Phase we begin with activities using paper and cardboard.

Cutting, folding and joining activities with paper

Lightweight paper that is easily cut can be used as a flat piece, or the paper can be folded one or more times before being cut.

Paper can be folded into tiny squares, and then cut. When unfolded, many detailed patterns are revealed.

Paper can be cut into various lengths and strips. These can be overlapped, folded together, curved into a circle, and stapled or glued.

Coloured paper can be cut into shapes and used to make a 'picture' by pasting the pieces on to a large piece of paper or card.

Make a paper mosaic

Select a variety of papers with different colours, textures, thicknesses and so on. Sort them, cut or tear them, then paste them on to a sheet of paper to create a paper mosaic.

Free-standing models

Cardboard can be folded, cut and joined to make free-standing models which can be quickly changed, taken apart or added to.

Stuffed-paper figures

Brown wrapping paper or white butcher's paper can be used to make large animals, people and other creatures that can be stuffed and closed. A shape is cut and matched with an identical shape. The edges are pinned or stapled together leaving an opening for the stuffing.

Paper and cardboard masks

Masks can be constructed out of paper bags, paper plates, construction paper or cardboard. A basic mask can be constantly changed by adding paper, wool, fabric and other 'stick on' bits and pieces.

Puppets

Paper-bag puppets are easy and inexpensive to make, and they are adaptable. The bag can be used in two ways. The base end has a flap that becomes a mouth OR the flattened end of the bag can fold over and a face can be drawn on the flat bottom of the bag. Paper cups or cereal boxes can also be made into puppets.

Foil shapes

Aluminium foil can be squeezed to make a shape. Wire, feathers and other decorative pieces can be added.

Discussion

Encourage the children to discuss what they have made with others at various stages during the process. Techniques can be refined, effects highlighted and the meaning enhanced. It is important therefore that constructed pieces do not become fixed or permanent too soon.

Tell us about your model.

Is it something real?

Can you tell us a story about it?

Does it have a name/title?

Questions may be asked to clarify content.

Which is the most important part?

Can you explain this a bit more?

Tell us more about this part.

Techniques can be highlighted through questioning.

How did you join these pieces?

Did you cut parts?

Will your model stand? How?

Crafting and Presenting

The children could construct:
- a piece as part of a play or story; for example, a hat, mask, costume, OR write a story based on the piece created
- models using paper and cardboard; for example, stuffed-paper creatures, paper-bag puppets, a robot or suit of armour from cardboard boxes and pieces
- using specified techniques; for example, folding, fringing, crumpling, pleating
- models to illustrate an event/outing or something related to a classroom theme in other learning areas such as Science, Maths, Language and Literature, Social Studies, Music, Drama
- classroom environmental spaces; for example, a shop, a cubby for quiet writing/reading.

CONSTRUCTION
Phase 2

LEARNING OBJECTIVES

1 Children will explore and discover the potential of a variety of papers, cardboards and plastics as construction materials.
2 Children will use a variety of construction techniques to make basic forms for models and structures.
3 Children will construct environmental spaces using collected materials.
4 Children will create texture by techniques such as perforating or attaching pieces to the surface of a structure.
5 Children will extend their techniques to include a variety of joining methods.
6 Children will evaluate and modify a structure as it is developed.
7 Children will become familiar with language relating to construction: cardboard, cover paper, tissue, cellophane, structure, sculpture, sculptor, top, seal, sphere, cone, cylinder, strip, prism, curling, scoring, mobile, costume, prop, slit, slot, punch, clip.

LEARNING EXPERIENCES

Getting Started

Examine containers

Examine collections of containers made of paper, cardboard, plastic and polystyrene. Observe how they are made, the materials used for joining, their function and use.

Collect construction materials

Encourage the children to collect materials from home that can be used for construction. Collect different types of paper, card, boxes and plastic containers.

Increase the children's awareness of personal spaces (home, school, playground, classroom, my room) by discussing size, arrangement of furniture, amount of unused space, size of articles in the space and so on.

Use the collected materials to create environmental spaces in the classroom.

Study structures

Ask the children to cut pictures from magazines or newspapers of various structures and display them in the classroom or paste them in a class book. Observe the many ways the same object is structured. Captions can be written to accompany the pictures: a book of bridges, buildings around the world, statues and sculptures.

This becomes a catalogue of ideas.

Experiment with forms

Experiment with several basic forms which can be made with paper and cardboard: circles, spheres, cones, cylinders, irregular shapes, rectangles, squares, strips, prisms.

'Quick' constructions

Incorporate a variety of construction activities as quick problem-solving experiences: folding cardboard to stand upright, making a bridge without using tape or glue to join, making a tall tower with boxes, making a wide model.

Change constructions

Encourage children to change a construction—by adding another piece, taking away, moving sections.

Card houses

Make temporary structures using playing cards.

Developing Concepts and Techniques

The ideas and techniques in Phase 1 for working with simple construction materials such as paper and cardboard are developed further in this Phase.

Activities are designed to refine and extend the children's existing techniques.

Perforate paper surfaces for texture

Flat sheets of paper can be cut at repeated intervals to create a textured surface. After the flat sheet has been perforated with a pleasing design pattern, it can be rolled into a cone or folded to create a three-dimensional structure.

Curl and score paper

Paper cut into strips can be curled by wrapping it around a pencil or cylinder.

Light paper can be scored by pressing and dragging open scissors along the strip.

Paper can also be scored by placing a ruler along its surface and then lightly cutting into it with the point of the scissors. The crease or fold can then be done with ease.

Make masks and costumes

Simple masks can be made by perforating, rolling, fringing and curling sheets of paper. Simple costumes can be made by using butcher's paper or large paper bags as a foundation. They can be decorated by pasting on pieces of brightly coloured cloth, paper or wool. Fringed paper or paper strips, shapes and other cut or folded forms can also be added.

Activities with cardboard

Using cones, cylinders, egg cartons, corrugated cardboard, make temporary constructions, then change and modify them.

Make different shapes by cutting cones, cylinders or egg cartons in two, three or four pieces and joining them in different ways.

Make a structure using corrugated cardboard. Use match sticks poked into the corrugations and tapes to join the strips. For instance, you could make a bridge or boat pier from corrugated cardboard. Design the supports so that the construction can carry weight.

Build with boxes

Use a variety of boxes to make a model which can be taken apart. Change and modify the model.

Combine a variety of small boxes with masking tape or cellotape to construct a model.

Combine boxes with threads or strings or paper clips.

Join boxes using glue to make a model and decorate the outside with coloured paper.

Build with plastics

Use plastic bottles and containers to make temporary constructions. Cut plastic containers with scissors and join with masking tape to make models.

String plastic lids together to make a mobile and decorate.

Discussion

Discussion of the children's constructed pieces will lead to revision and refinement. Sharing time during the process may proceed through questions such as:

What is your piece about?

Does your model have a name?

Show us your model from different angles.

Can you tell us more about this part?

Could you add anything to the piece?

Is there any part you would like to change?

Is there a part you could use in another piece?

Did you use a technique you could use in another piece?

Crafting and Presenting

The children could construct:

- masks, costumes and props as part of a play or story
- models using paper, cardboard and plastics

Stick or rod puppets

A rod puppet is extended on a stick and worked from below. Heads for stick puppets can be made from a variety of scrap materials such as paper cups and plates, small boxes, old tennis balls, polystyrene, corn husks, food containers and cans.

Egg-carton constructions

Make caterpillars or alligators.

- models to illustrate ideas across curriculum areas
- using a specified joining technique; for example, gluing, taping, stringing together
- mobiles from lightweight objects
- musical instruments such as cymbals, drums, bells and chimes, shakers and rattles, rhythm sticks
- environmental spaces relating to a classroom theme or subject area; for example, 'Our neighbourhood', 'Our School' (Social Studies). Construct cities from books and stories; for example, the Land of Oz. Construct fairy-tale castles with kings and queens.

CONSTRUCTION
Phase 3

LEARNING OBJECTIVES

1 Children will use a variety of materials (and tools) for construction.
2 Children will employ a variety of joining techniques for construction.
3 Children will gain confidence in their employment of techniques and show a willingness to discuss appropriate uses of them.
4 Children will explore and discover the constructional possibilities of wood and polystyrene.
5 Children will learn the techniques of working with papier-mâché.
6 Children will become familiar with language relating to construction: wood, mallet, hammer, nails, vice, plane, screwdriver, file, chisel, saw, knife, drill, sandpaper, polish, wood finish, wax, varnish, foam, pin, nail, papier-mâché, pinata, interior, exterior, design, plan, scale, space.

LEARNING EXPERIENCES

Getting Started

Look at masks

Use a display of pictures and photographs of rituals and ceremonies from societies throughout the world. Masks and costumes have always been part of these rituals; they help the wearer to ward off evil spirits, bring rain, drive away disease, tell stories and so on. Study these masks both past and present. Emphasize that they are common to many cultures.

Look at the use of papier-mâché for festival masks and ritual objects. Many commercial products from China, Japan and Mexico also utilize papier-mâché.

Look at sculpture

Make a display of pieces sculpted from wood, stone, plaster, metal, china or glass.

Visit an art gallery to view the sculptures or a park to view monuments and statues.

View objects in the round

Encourage the children to view various three-dimensional forms from several angles: front, side, bottom and top. Viewing should be a continuous process. Touching, handling, moving, changing and re-arranging should also be encouraged (though not in art galleries!).

Collect construction materials

Children can bring cardboard boxes and rolls, egg cartons, polystyrene, newspapers and magazines, pieces of wood and scrap materials. These can be sorted for use in various constructions.

Talk about environmental spaces

Increase the children's awareness of environmental spaces through discussion of the home, school, neighbourhood and so on.

Draw plans and maps of personal spaces. Look at magazines showing new ideas for homes and beautiful living environments. Very often they include simple diagrams and floor-plan drawings. The magazines are helpful because they show the finished photograph of the completed structure, as well as the plans for them.

Developing Concepts and Techniques

As the range of materials increases, encourage the children to explore materials 'open-endedly'—that is, to discover what the material can do and what can happen as the forms are developed without preconceived images and final products. In the process the children 'play around'; they assemble, take apart, and try new formations and structures. The discoveries made through these quick construction activities are important. Encourage the children to record successful ideas for future reference. The materials outlined in the previous stages (paper, cardboard, plastic) are also used in this Phase to refine previously learned techniques. However, other materials are also introduced to allow the development of new ideas and techniques.

Introduce wood

Discover what can be done with wood: pound it, scratch it, poke tools into it. Use simple tools such as gouges, mallets, hammers and nails, chisels, saws and dull knives.

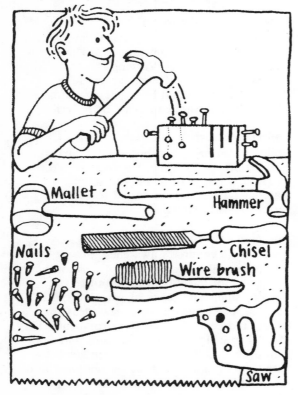

Use tools with wood

Discover the use of tools.

Mark lines on a piece of wood and saw to varying depths (without sawing right through).

Draw a line pattern on the wood, then hammer nails into the wood following the pattern.

Draw a pattern or shape on the wood and drill holes of various sizes following the shape.

Texture and finish

Texture can be created by rubbing with: sandpaper, a wire brush, a hard object such as a stone, bone or piece of glass.

Finish the surface of the wood by rubbing or painting with: shoe polish, floor wax, oil, crayons, paint, varnish.

Work with polystyrene

Carve foam pieces with nails or knives, or cut with scissors to shape pieces.

Join pieces by gluing or by using pins, nails or tooth picks.

String pieces together (to make mobiles).

Work with papier-mâché

Use preformed shapes to support the papier mâché. Plastic bottles, bowls, ice-cream containers, aluminium foil, polystyrene, paper milk cartons, small jars and cans make solid supports and are light enough to leave inside the construction. Balloons make excellent foundations for masks. Polystyrene trays or cardboard box lids are excellent for creating wall plaques.

Some points to remember with papier-mâché

1 Newspaper has a grain, therefore rip the paper from the fold down. It should then tear easily and in straight strips.
2 Apply strips firmly but avoid wetting the form too much.
3 Use white towelling or plain newsprint for the last coat.
4 Keep the paint thick enough to cover the finished form. A small amount of white glue added to the paint will prevent cracking.
5 Allow enough time for thorough drying (2 days) so the paint does not crack after it dries. Place the object over a bottle or sit it in a box or bucket for drying.
6 Secure the legs or appendages to the body of a construction with tape, wire or string, so they will not pull apart.
7 If the model is to be hung or carried, it should be kept light. For free-standing models, heavier supports can be introduced.

Discussion

The children should be encouraged to discuss their ideas, how the piece developed and the techniques and methods used. Sharing for responses leads naturally to the changing or extending of pieces. The children's efforts — to expand and specify, subtract or add pieces, use a different method or technique or reject the piece and begin again — can be highlighted through questioning.

What is your piece about?

How long have you been working on the piece?

What was your initial idea?

How did the piece develop?

What is the most important part of the piece?

How did you show this?

How do you think others will feel when they view the piece?

Crafting and Presenting

The children could construct:
- using a variety of materials and methods
- using combinations of materials and techniques; for example, puppets, toys and mobiles can be made using a variety of collectable materials and techniques of construction
- to integrate with other learning areas such as Science, Maths, Language and Literature, Social Studies, Music and Drama
- using papier-mâché to create masks, puppets, dolls, sculptures, figures and mobiles such as a pinata

Pinatas

A pinata is a container filled with lollies or gifts and covered with papier-mâché.
It can be in the form of an animal, ball, star or other, original shape.
Fringed coloured paper is glued on in layers to cover the shape.
The pinata is hung from the ceiling and the children are blindfolded and take turns trying to break it with a stick.

- wooden models that will stand on their own
- polystyrene sculptured pieces (animals, cars, trains)
- projects related to space design (in a group); for example, personal environments, ('My dream house', 'A superspace playground'), community environments (a shopping plaza, a children's park and zoo), imaginative spaces (a space city of the future, places from books and stories).

CONSTRUCTION
Phase 4

LEARNING OBJECTIVES

1 Children will use a variety of techniques, materials and tools for construction.
2 Children will select appropriate construction materials and techniques to suit specific purposes.
3 Children will explore and discover the constructional possibilities of wire.
4 Children will plan and develop a piece (including evaluating a design, making changes and deciding on a final structure) and present it to an audience.
5 Children will become familiar with language relating to construction: wire, bend, twist, loop, curl, wrap, pliers, coil, roll, wire, cutters, tin snips, armature, three-dimensional, architect, interior decorator, draftsman, town planning officer, demolition, carve, balance, strength, rigid, support, girders, tower, bridge, piles, posts.

LEARNING EXPERIENCES

Getting Started

Look at structures through the ages

Look at the great sculptures from ancient civilizations such as the Greeks and discuss the tools and methods used to create them. Compare these ancient materials and methods with contemporary sculptures made from new materials such as plastics and steel.

How did various tools affect structures in the past?

What tools are available today as compared to the past?

How did lifestyles and cultures affect structures, and vice versa?

Invite a guest speaker

Invite an architect, town planning officer, interior designer, draftsperson or sculptor to your classroom to talk about their crafts/professions.

Visit structures

Visit various areas to view constructions such as outdoor sculptures, renewal areas, a building under construction, an area under demolition.

Observe architectural details and styles through excursions or photos.

Discuss change

Discuss the idea of change in the environment. Ask questions such as:

What do you like about our city/school?

What would you like to change?

How could you change it?

Draw maps and layouts to show this change.

Look at famous structures

Discuss the Eiffel Tower, the Empire State Building, the Sydney Harbour Bridge and so on. Ask questions such as:

What is the purpose of the structure?

What does it do?

Why have the building?

What do you do in it?

Visit a gallery

Consider the sculptured pieces.

How do you feel when you look at it?

Is it pleasing to the eye?

What message do you think the artist is trying to display?

Is the sculpture balanced?

What materials did the artist use?

What tools do you think the artist used?

Do you think the material used suits the subject matter?

Why or why not?

Is the piece beautiful, useful, expressive?

Developing Concepts and Techniques

Children in this Phase must be provided with learning experiences that present a challenge. Problem-solving situations with a variety of construction materials encourage the children to make choices and decisions about content, materials and techniques. Children in this Phase need to search out three-dimensional materials and, through selecting, experimenting and manipulating, work through a plan to a new form. Many ideas can be thought out in advance and these can be explored through drawing sketches and making small trial models.

The process involved in making mobiles, toys, musical instruments, kites or any similar model becomes a problem-solving situation as the children question themselves.

What qualities am I trying to achieve?

What aesthetic qualities of the object am I trying to achieve?

What materials match these desired qualities?

What is the durability and availability (cost) of these materials?

What techniques do I need to use?

Is it useful to make preliminary sketches?

Making puppets can also become a problem-solving situation. Because we have only two hands and ten fingers, we need to decide which parts of the puppet we will want to have move. This, in turn, will determine the type of puppet construction children will select.

Does the mouth move?

Do the hands, arms or ears move?

Does the whole puppet move, as with a rod puppet or marionette?

Do the legs move to walk and dance?

Much of the thrill and surprise in puppet-making is in the creation and discovery of what will take place. It is difficult to decide which activity is more fun—inventing the

character, or operating and manipulating it.

As in the previous Phases the children use common materials such as paper, cardboard, plastic, wood and polystyrene to refine and reinforce ideas and techniques of construction. However, new materials can be introduced.

Activities with wire

Use a variety of lengths and weights of wire to experiment with methods of shaping and twisting wire. Achieve effects by beginning at and working out from the centre core or support. Shapes can be built up with solid masses of wire wrapped around or kept open by using single strands of wire.

Use old scissors or pliers as tools to bend, twist, loop, curl, wrap and join the wires.

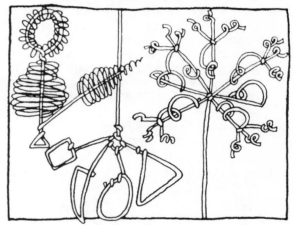

Line design boards: string art

Make a line by connecting pairs of points (in this case, stretched string to nails hammered into a board) so that the design appears to be a curved shape.

Good line designs require skill in measurement, organization and planning.

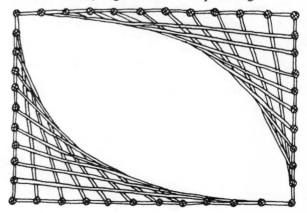

Discuss linear and three-dimensional forms

Discuss how the forms created with wire and string are linear, like a drawing. That is, they are composed of lines. By interlacing the lines a three-dimensional form can be created.

Discuss what it means to form a three-dimensional design that has length, height and width. It can be constructed into a whole from parts or from a whole by taking parts away. It can be modelled with soft materials, or carved from firm materials.

Carving

Introduce children to the idea of constructing from a whole piece by carving.

Polystyrene, wax or soap can be carved with a nail or small screwdriver or wood-carving tools. Encourage the children to turn the piece often to consider its three-dimensional surfaces. Carved pieces can be joined by inserting toothpicks into them.

Gourds provide experience in planning designs that go around a surface. After cutting they can be painted, dyed and waxed, or left as they are.

Discussion

As the children become familiar with the various uses of materials and techniques, they can experiment with partial pieces, evaluate a design, discuss how the piece will develop and decide on the best direction to take. The teacher's role is to offer encouragement and support to guide the children through the process.

These questions may be asked before beginning the piece.

What will my piece be (about)?

How will I begin?

Do I need more information; for example, should I draw a preliminary sketch?

What materials should I use?

What methods and techniques should I use?

As the piece develops, the following questions help the children to re-evaluate and move forward.

Which part is showing the most promise?

How can I build on this?

What do I need to change?

Will this suit the intended meaning of the piece?

What techniques do I need to use now?

Finally further self-evaluation can occur through questions such as:

Does the audience understand it/enjoy it?

How does my piece compare with my original plan?

Is there something here that I could use again?

How does this compare with my other pieces?

Crafting and Presenting

The children could construct:
- toys from collectable materials
- mobiles and kites from lightweight parts
- a variety of puppets, including hand puppets, puppets with papier-mâché heads, paper-bag or paper-cup puppets, finger puppets, stick or rod puppets, marionettes
- a model following a plan or sketch
- a piece using a set of instructions, plan or sketch thought out in advance
- wire structures as armatures (frameworks) for: papier-mâché, buildings, towers, bridges
- wire and string designs (figures, animals) to stand on their own
- objects from soap, wax or polystyrene by carving.

REFERENCES

Allsop, David. Echuca Art Committee. *Inklings*. Echuca District Education Committee Publications, Tongala, 1981.

Bendigo District Education Committee, Art Sub-committee. 'An Art Resource for Primary Teachers'. Loddon Campaspe–Mallee Regional Office, Education Department, Bendigo, 1982.

Cambourne, Brian. 'Seven Conditions for Translating Language Learning Theory into Classroom Practice'. Primary English Teachers' Association, English Teachers' Association Conference, 1983.

Eisner, Earl W. *Educating Artistic Vision*. Macmillan, Melbourne, 1972.

Education Department of Victoria. *Course of Study for Primary Schools: Art and Craft*. Melbourne, 1967.

Gaitskell, Charles D. & Hurwitz, Al. *Children and their Art: Methods for the Elementary School*. 3rd edn, Harcourt Brace Jovanovich, New York, 1975.

Hart, Kate, Geisler, Jutta & Emblin, Di. *I Can Draw: A Resource Book of 2-D Activities for Primary Teachers*. Ringwood Resource Centre.

Linderman, Earl W. and Linderman, Marlene M. *Arts and Crafts for the Classroom*. 2nd edn, Macmillan, New York, 1984.

McPherson, Heather. *Ideas for Art and Craft*. Nelson, Melbourne, 1981.

Richardson, Donald. *Introducing Art: A First Book on the History and Appreciation of the Visual Arts*. Longman Cheshire, Melbourne, 1983.

Rowe, Gaelene & Lomas, Bill. *A Writing Curriculum: Process and Conference*. Oxford University Press, Melbourne, 1984.

Warragul Catholic Education Office, Art Study Group. *Art Base: A Basic Guideline for Art in the Primary School: Printmaking*. Warragul, 1985.

Wilson, Larry (comp.). *An Art Course for Primary Schools*. Stawell Inspectorate, 1979.